THE IRONIES OF WAR

An Introduction to Homer's *Iliad*

Ian C. Johnston

UNIVERSITY
PRESS OF
AMERICA

Lanham • New York • London

Copyright © 1988 by

University Press of America,® Inc.

4720 Boston Way
Lanham, MD 20706

3 Henrietta Street
London WC2E 8LU England

Printed in the United States of America

British Cataloging in Publication Information Available

Library of Congress Cataloging-in-Publication Data

Johnston, Ian C., 1938–
The ironies of war : an introduction to Homer's Iliad / by Ian C. Johnston.
p. cm. Bibliography: p. Includes index.
1. Homer. Iliad. 2. War in literature. 3. Irony in literature.
4. Trojan War in literature. I. Title.
PA4037.J58   1988
883'.01—dc 19   88–14861 CIP
ISBN 0–8191–7029–1 (alk. paper)

All University Press of America books are produced on acid-free
paper which exceeds the minimum standards set by the National
Historical Publications and Records Commission.

To My Mother

Acknowledgements

I wish thank the Malaspina College Board for giving me the opportunity to take a six-month sabbatical leave in 1987. Without such generous support I would not have had the time to complete this book.

I also owe a debt of gratitude to Peter Hoemberg for his unfailingly helpful advice on the mysteries of word processing and for his invaluable assistance in preparing the manuscript for publication.

Table of Contents

CHAPTER 1

Introduction

We seek first to discover how Homer (or Shakespeare, or Michelangelo, or Beethoven, or Rodin) achieves his dominion over us; how he has himself attained to his own art and mystery of craftsmanship, to that outlook over things which he communicates to us, to that mastery of what lies under his hand which makes all things new when that hand has passed over them. Yet to discover this is but the revenue side of the critic's account with him. On the opposite page of that account is the use which we may make of that analysis, that reasoned account of our experience, for the enlargement, disentanglement and articulation of our own experience and the training of our own native ability. So we may begin to see things as Homer or Shakespeare saw them, and be, in our own outlook and our rendering of it in expression, ourselves more Homeric, more Shakespearean, more nearly master-craftsmen in the supreme art of living well, in the twentieth century. (Sir John Myres)

I

To begin with the traditional question: Why another introductory book on Homer's *Iliad*, another entry into a crowded field? Given the many extant studies of the epic, the reader is entitled to an answer that will either whet his appetite for what follows or spare him the trouble of proceeding much further. For, like any great work of art, the *Iliad* means different things to different people: the historian, philologist, literary critic, psychologist, archeologist, literary historian, student of religion, expert in mythology--each brings to books on the *Iliad* different expectations and desires. Since no single critical study can possibly satisfy all these interests and since I have a purpose in some ways rather different from other introductions, it is just as well to clarify matters right at the start.

I address this essay primarily to readers who are meeting the *Iliad* for the first time and in an English translation and who are chiefly inter-

1

ested in the poem as an enduring literary classic. A few more experienced readers of the *Iliad* may find the essay useful and, perhaps, stimulating, here and there, but my main concern is those readers relatively new to Homer, members of the general public and students still attending classes in high school and university. About such readers I have made a number of basic assumptions which have shaped this introduction. Given the fact that translations of Homer's epic remain very popular in an age when the traditional commitment to full-time Classical Studies and the knowledge of ancient cultures which that fosters have almost disappeared among senior school students and undergraduates, I start from the obvious fact that many readers of the *Iliad*, almost certainly the majority, bring to the poem no special knowledge of or interest in Homer's original language and, for the most part, almost no informed opinions about Ancient Greek history or culture. Few have the intention of pursuing Classical Studies any further than, at best, a short course, self-directed or otherwise, in selected readings of works in translation. Consequently, many of those reading the *Iliad* nowadays approach the text as a great classic which they can appreciate in a modern translation without a detailed knowledge of the original Greek or of the historical moment when the poem first appeared. Furthermore, largely on the basis of my experience as a teacher of Classical literature in translation, I assume that, although many contemporary readers may lack even a rudimentary historical or linguistic background, they often do bring qualities essential for an appreciation of the *Iliad*: a lively imagination, a demonstrated interest in reading, a knowledge of English literature, and a great desire to discover the poetic richness of what they have heard is one of their culture's great books. This essay addresses such readers before all others and sets out to assist them in their first experience of the poem.

The most important single difference between this introduction to the *Iliad* and almost all the others available in the book stores and libraries is the central insistence here on treating the *Iliad* in translation as a poem immediately accessible to the imagination of the contemporary reader. I do not mean to assert that the *Iliad* presents no difficulties or that we can ignore the fact that it is the product of a culture very different in many respects from our own; on the contrary, the epic constantly challenges the reader's interpretative responses and his modern sensibility in a manner that few other works of fiction can manage. Indeed, therein lies much of its value to us. However, treating the English text of the *Iliad* as a work which the modern reader can grasp without the constant assistance of historical scholarship assumes that the reader, as an interpreter of the poem, has within him the resources to deal with the strangeness in Homer's vision and that the commentator's first responsibility must be to help the reader recognize his own imaginative

2

potential for experiencing the ancient poem rather than to lead him away from the text into pre-requisite studies of historical matters.

This claim, of course, introduces a well-known and controversial debate, for the arguments about the conflicting demands of historical scholarship and contemporary interpretation go back at least as far as the beginnings of modern criticism. I have no desire here to rehearse those arguments, but I should point out my own view that, for a number of different reasons, the tradition of introducing Homer's poem through the details of the historical period of its composition and transmission or of the represented fiction can often affect the interpretative process in a manner not always very helpful to the reader, especially the inexperienced student. To say this is not by any means to denigrate historical scholarship but simply to insist that the interpretation of a text is, in many important ways, an activity significantly different from research into its origins and that an undue emphasis upon historical matters, of the sort very common in almost all introductions to the *Iliad*, can have the unfortunate tendency of erecting barriers between the reader and the text and, more important, of persuading him that any imaginative unease the poem may generate in his modern sensibilities can be excused on the ground that the poem deals with an ancient, obscure, and therefore no longer particularly relevant vision of experience. Furthermore, such an emphasis on a preliminary study of the history of the poem as a necessary approach to the text can also contradict our experiences as readers.

> The search for the author's generative intention as context of the poem is a search for a temporal moment which must, as the author and poem live on, recede and ever recede into the forgotten, as all moments do. Poems, on this theory of their meaning, must always steadily grow less and less correctly known and knowable; they must dwindle in meaning and being toward a vanishing point. The best known and most valuable poem must be that written but a moment ago--and its best or only possible audience must be the author. But poems we know are not really like that. The most self-assured authors publish their works and hang upon public recognition. Shakespeare has more meaning and value now than he had in his own day. There is a sense in which even Homer, though we construe his language with pain and are not sure how many persons he was, has more meaning and is more valuable today than ever before. (Wimsatt 276)

In this essay, therefore, I shift the customary emphasis in introductions to Homer, by encouraging the reader to recognize in a translation of the *Iliad* a vision of human experience which can speak directly to him, if he will honestly and openly confront the strange power of the text, bringing to it his own contemporary sensibility, prejudices and all, and allow the text to challenge them and be challenged by them. For on its ability to speak directly to the imagination from one age to the next, to bring to bear an ancient vision of man upon the emotional sensibilities of a later time, and to produce a significant response in the interaction between the new reader and the text, on that poetic power above all else, it seems to me, rests the greatness of the *Iliad*. My goal here is to promote that unmediated interaction, a conversation, if you will, between the reader and Homer's English text, by offering a sustained interpretative essay which does not attempt to fragment the initial experience of the poem into historical rubrics and which strives as much as possible to avoid the specialized languages of much contemporary literary criticism and history. Whether I succeed or not, the reader will have to judge for himself; in these matters the value of the critical practice depends not upon the skill with which I can muster a theoretical defense of a particular methodology but rather upon the extent to which my observations enrich an understanding of the poem and, beyond that, stimulate the reader to generate fresh insights of his own.

I am aware of some of the objections to this approach. It may be true, as G. S. Kirk observes, that Homer did not design the *Iliad* to withstand a close examination (*Songs* 351). Nevertheless, the *Iliad*, like Shakespeare's plays, about which one might make a similar claim, can sustain detailed reading; indeed, the enduring popularity of the epic among academic critics and general readers surely demonstrates the fact. Then, too, the issues which arise from any approach which rests upon the close reading of a modern English text may well raise objections about the validity of such use of a translation. Without attempting to address this problem, I take the common sense view that a good English translation, while clearly not exactly the same as the original, still qualifies as Homer's poem or, more strictly speaking, a version of it; for if it is not Homer, then what is it? Surely not just another pretty poem.

A second difference between this introductory study of the *Iliad* and most others follows naturally from the first. Since my aim is to place the epic, not in its historical period, but right in the centre of the modern reader's contemporary consciousness, I frequently direct his attention to those areas of his experience of fact and fiction which may assist him in seeing more clearly what is going on in an often very disturbing and apparently alien picture of human life. Consequently, this interpretation of the *Iliad* often draws comparisons between Homer's epic and Shakespeare's plays, Milton's *Paradise Lost*, modern fictions (including films), and those features of the reader's culture which may render Homer's epic more accessible to him. I recognize a danger in this process, since obviously it may at times, in a search for relevance, lose sight of the significant differences between the Iliadic warriors, Shakespeare's characters, and modern Western society. Still, properly controlled comparisons of all sorts are not only legitimate tools of the literary critic but also an essential means of overcoming the new reader's sometimes considerable reluctance to turn his complete imaginative attention onto a poem that at first can appear so forbiddingly old and strange. For the *Iliad*, even in modern English, can intimidate the reader, especially the unsure student, its unique and alien power stifling his ability to respond as fully as he might, and whatever the interpreter can draw upon to overcome this difficulty, without in the process distorting the poem or leading the reader away from the text, is useful.

II

This essay has a relatively simple form. To begin with, Chapter 2 examines the most obvious and most important feature of the poem, namely, the war. For the *Iliad* is our first and greatest war story, and if we wish to explore the epic in any detail we have to examine carefully the central way of life it presents. To affix the label "War Fiction" to a text, of course, is to say relatively little about it, for there is probably a greater variety in the fictional treatment of war than in any other popular narrative genre. Hence the initial need for a particularly close scrutiny of Homer's world of combat. By comparing that vision with some modern accounts, in fiction and non-fiction, and our different reactions to them, I stress that the strangeness we may experience in reading the *Iliad* comes not so much from the time separating us from the Ancient Greeks nor from any unfamiliarity with the conventions of oral epic, odd as these may often at first appear, but from the ways in which we have been educated to respond to warfare, that is, from our modern cultural prejudices. The *Iliad* is a powerful poem because it strikes a very responsive chord in the modern reader; at the same time, however, it can be disturbing and even repellent to the reader who does not recognize, or who does not want to recognize, that note coming from his own psyche. The ancient work, in other words, puts him in touch with a permanently vital part of himself, but a part that he would often prefer not to acknowledge.

Once the reader recognizes the obviously central importance of the war and begins to see clearly Homer's picture of it, then a great deal of the epic becomes immediately much more familiar. Consequently, Chapter 3 (Nature and the Gods), Chapter 4 (The Heroic Code), Chapter 5 (Arms and the Men), and Chapter 6 (The *Iliad* as a Tragedy: The Warrior, the Victim, and the Tragic Hero) examine the ways in which an initial appreciation of Homer's vision of combat can provide an imaginative entry into many different aspects of the epic. Throughout I try to link the discussion of particular points as much as possible to detailed consideration of specific passages from the text, in the belief that this method will encourage the reader to direct a keener eye at the entire poem. The concluding section, Chapter 7 (Homer and the Modern Imagination), argues for the continuing importance of Homer's vision, especially in a very different age, on the assumption that a view of human life outside our own contemporary mythologies can best illuminate for us what we have become. In addition, Chapter 7 calls attention to some of the ways in which those contemporary mythologies have systematically led many writers on the *Iliad* to misinterpret Homer's view of warfare and thus more or less seriously to distort the poem.

A word about the critical method in this essay. Central to my exploration of the *Iliad* is the very familiar notion of irony as a means by which in a complex work the reader's response to what is happening undergoes a constant re-evaluation throughout. Hence, the title of the essay. In this sense, the irony in Homer requires us always to adjust and then to readjust our reactions to the characters and the events, as we recognize that the vision of life is not so straightforward as it may at first reading appear. The irony forcibly reminds us that what we witness in the *Iliad* is complex and ambiguous. For if Homer's vision of warfare is obviously important, it is by no means simple. To appreciate the *Iliad* properly thus requires the reader to confront a constant pressure to examine his understanding of the war and of those whose lives are based upon it, so that by the end he cannot easily sum up the precise vision of war which Homer offers. The *Iliad*, in other words, like Shakespeare's plays, has a characteristic ambiguity.

> Yet by the end we have been through a constantly turbulent experience which demands an incessant giving and taking back of allegiance, a counterpoint of ever-shifting response to phrase, speech, character, scene, action, a welter of emotions and ideas and perceptions and surprises and intuitions of underlying unity and coherence rivalled only by our experience in the real world so perplexingly suggested by the artifact to which we yield ourselves. The attempt to state the meaning of the play is not much more likely to produce an accurate account than an attempt to state the meaning of life. But to say that we cannot profitably talk about the meaning of life is not to say that life is meaningless. (Rabkin 104)

In this sense, Homer's picture is thoroughly ironic; his poem forces the reader to take into account the full human and metaphysical complexity of a disturbing vision of human experience, and because that vision is so different in many respects from our own, reading the *Iliad* presents unique difficulties (the *Odyssey*, by contrast, strikes us as much more immediately congenial, not because the *Odyssey* lacks irony but rather because its ironies register as obviously more familiar). A common early response to a partial first reading of the *Iliad*, especially among undergraduates, is to applaud or to denigrate the poem as a simple pro- or anti-war piece. There are many passages which a propagandist for either cause might well use in isolation. Indeed, my first acquaintance with Homer came when, as a teenager, in an abandoned prospector's camp

in Northern Ontario I stumbled across a little manual of poetry special-
ly published for soldiers departing for the front lines. The selections,
Homer prominent among them, were obviously designed to fill the
reader with enthusiasm for the most aggressive military behaviour.
Homer's ironic treatment of the war, however, renders simplistic any
such attempt to place the *Iliad* as an artistic totality firmly on the side of
the doves or of the hawks.

I should make clear, however, that I do not push the notion of irony
to the point where it disallows the evaluative judgment. A good deal of
fashionable literary criticism nowadays would have it that the ironies and
ambiguities of artistic metaphor and language generally are so pervasive
and powerful that the interpreter's task is simply to call attention, often
with as much rhetorical flourish as possible, to the ways in which the language contradicts itself and thus renders any notion of a coherent vision
quite vain. If, as J. Hillis Miller claims, "A critic must choose either the
tradition of presence [i.e. significant meaning] or the tradition of 'difference' [i.e. contradiction], for their assumptions about language, about
literature, about history, and about the mind cannot be made compatible" (qtd Leitch 593)[1], then I declare my faith in the old belief that
great books, like the *Iliad*, are about something which, for want of a better expression, we might call "life" and that the critic's first task is to bring
his interpretative judgment to bear upon the work and, inevitably therefore, also upon the contemporary cultural prejudices which inform his
own thinking. William Empson's statement that everyone is on trial in a
civilized narrative has always struck me as extremely useful common-
sense advice to the reader, for it points his attention at once onto what
remains central to a work's modern importance and holds at bay many
intriguing and complex digressions.

I recognize that this critical stance is not particularly fashionable any
more in some quarters, but I make no apology for that. The mimetic
tradition in literary criticism, the claim that literature presents some vital
assertions about the human condition and that the rights and responsibilities of the interpreter include, above all else, the detailed evaluation
of those assertions and of the judgments we find ourselves making upon

1   So far as I am aware, the deconstructive method of interpretation has not yet infected
    Classical Studies to the extent that it has other areas of literary inquiry. An example
    of interest to readers of the Iliad does occur in Paul de Man's Blindness and Insight,
    in a passage where the author endeavors to demonstrate by this critical method that
    Homer's war epic has no connection whatsoever to any coherent reality. For a
    description of de Man's comments and an appropriately sensible rejoinder, see Graff
    173-5.

them, is our oldest and most valuable source of literary insights, largely because, for all the limitations one might point to in this or that piece of mimetic criticism, it meets the most urgent needs of the reader whose primary interest in a work is its contemporary relevance to his own life rather than its position in the historical, syntactical, or typological scheme of things and, beyond that, because it permits the ancient vision to work upon him as it should, to educate him into a better understanding of how he thinks and feels.

> [The process of interpretation] does this by provoking my prejudices into consciousness and, by placing them under question, suspending their action as prejudices. But what holds my opinions under question is precisely the strange otherness of the challenging message. Hence what hermeneutic must consider as its "object" is not an object at all, but the relation between what is mine and what is other, between the present and the past, which initially bring each other into relief through contrast, and ultimately blend into each other through a mediation that expands one's horizons. (Kisiel 8)

III

In the following essay I have used Robert Fitzgerald's translation of the *Iliad* (Anchor, 1975). Unless otherwise stated all quotations from the *Iliad* come from this source. The quotes in this essay are from the most recent version of that paperback edition, which contains a number of major and minor revisions of the earlier text bearing the same date as the revised version. Since Fitzgerald departs from the strict lineation of the Greek text and therefore does not number his lines precisely, I include after each quote the appropriate specific reference for the first line of the quote, according to the Greek text of D. B. Munro (Oxford, 1896). In his translation Fitzgerald has departed from the traditional English spellings for many of the names (for example, Akhilleus, Akhaian, Hektor). For the sake of consistency, in my text I use Fitzgerald's spellings but without the accents he often employs.

The selection of Fitzgerald's translation rather than, say, Richard Lattimore's or E. V. Rieu's perhaps deserves a comment or two, since I am aware that many Homer scholars prefer them to Fitzgerald's. However, given my desire that readers should treat the *Iliad* in translation as a poem immediately accessible to their contemporary imaginations, the reasons for the choice are clear enough: Rieu's translation is very useful, but it suffers from the irremediable flaw (for my purposes) that it is written in prose, and Lattimore's translation, although much more faithful to the letter and form of the Greek text than either Rieu's or Fitzgerald's, too often displays a very unidiomatic English which seriously detracts from the quality of the poetry. I must stress that

Fitzgerald is not simply my favorite by default; whatever liberties he has taken with Homer's language and metre, Fitzgerald has, in my view, delivered the finest poetic translation of the *Iliad* in modern English. Indeed, such is my admiration for Fitzgerald's achievement that I would with confidence bestow upon it the lavish praise with which Fitzgerald himself greeted Lattimore's work: "Taste may change greatly, but it looks to me as if Mr. Lattimore's version would survive as long as Pope's for in its way is quite as solidly distinguished" ("Heroic Poems in English" 699).

Like every writer on Homer, I owe great debts to the work of many other literary and historical scholars and interpreters. I have tried as scrupulously as possible to acknowledge these obligations. However, in Homer criticism it is often very difficult to remember the source of a particular insight. Consequently, I may have unwittingly missed some important acknowledgements. Short of carrying out the (for me) impossible task of reading everything that has been written about Homer and filling the text with references, I can do little more than apologize in advance for any serious unintentional oversights.

CHAPTER 2

Homer's Vision of War

WAR: . . . sb. [Late OE. werre, a. ONF. werre (F. guerre), a. OHG. werra confusion, discord, strife, f. Teut. root *werz-, *wers-, whence also WORSE a.] 1. Hostile contention by means of armed forces, carried on between nations, states, or rulers, or between parties in the same nation or state; the employment of armed forces against a foreign power or against an opposing party in the state. Formerly freq. pl. in sing. sense. b. trans. and fig. Applied poet. or rhet. to any kind of active hostility or contention between living beings, or of conflict between opposing forces or principles ME. 2. A contest between armed forces carried on in a campaign or series of campaigns. (Often with identifying word or phrase, as in the Trojan War, the Wars of the Roses, the Thirty Years' War) ME. 3. Actual fighting; a battle, engagement (chiefly poet.) -1827. 4. The kind of operations by which the contention of armed forces is carried on; fighting as a department of activity, as a profession, or as an art. ME. 5. concr. Used poet. for: a. Instruments of war, munitions -1713. B. Soldiers in fighting array -1822. (Shorter Oxford English Dictionary)

My argument is that War makes rattling good history; but peace is poor reading. (Thomas Hardy)

I

The *Iliad* is, first and foremost, a war poem, our earliest, strangest, and greatest story of men in battle. The term is appropriate not just because a great deal of fighting takes place in the twenty-four books--about one third of the poem, over five thousand lines, concerns battles--nor because Homer repeatedly describes aspects of the warrior's life. In fact, the *Iliad* provides relatively few details of the practical realities of war, certainly far fewer than the historian of combat would like to find. But the phrase "war poem" offers a very useful starting point for a discussion of the epic, because the term introduces the central imaginative thrust of the fiction, the exploration of the conduct of human beings individually and collectively when they direct their energies into deadly combat. For the warfare in the *Iliad* does not serve as a merely incidental part of an exciting epic or dramatic narrative nor as a convenient backdrop for an action whose main focus falls elsewhere; the war in Homer's epic, from the opening lines to the very end, forms the organizing principle in a vision of human experience. The *Iliad*, in other words, is a war story in the same way that *War and Peace*, *For Whom the Bell Tolls*, *All Quiet on the Western Front*, and *Catch-22* are war stories and that, say, *Macbeth*, *Gone With the Wind*, and *From Here to Eternity*, for all their emphasis on battle scenes and soldiers, are not. We need not worry if this distinction sounds rather imprecise. The crucial point is that, however the reader wishes to enter the imaginative world of the *Iliad*, he should recognize from the start that he is dealing with men at war, constantly engaged in deadly combat, so the world of the fiction probably has little immediate similarity to his present surroundings.

Not that any student of modern culture lacks the opportunity to discover war. The subject has had a permanent appeal for writers and readers since Homer's time; indeed, with the possible exception of the trials and tribulations of young lovers, no subject has inspired popular writers more than warfare. Even our strenuous efforts in modern times to redirect or to suppress the imaginative appeal of war fictions has had little effect on altering the popularity of the tradition. Writers still find the subject as fascinating as ever[1], and as we plead with the young to give peace a chance, they nod in agreement and rush away to see Clint Eastwood in *Heartbreak Ridge*. The genre retains its hold on the popular imagination for obvious reasons. No other subject so plausibly allows the writer such a rich variety of different human behaviour. For the experience of war can include everything from long stretches of almost unbearable tedium, to moments of dashing romantic adventure, to intense joy, to roisterous or grotesque farce, to Grand Guignol horror, to incidents of the highest possible stress in which men test themselves in the face of imminent death. The switch from one state to the other can happen instantaneously, and the results are usually unpredictable. For warfare, in fact and in fiction, is the most ironic of human experiences: men set out to fight with certain attitudes, hopes, and fears, but the mortal combat brings out the unexpected. Brave soldiers go mad, nonentities become heroes, jingoist rhetoric transforms itself into revolting carnage, the peace-loving citizen turns butcher, lonely men discover the joys of comradeship, callow youths mature overnight, the unthinking grunt

---

1   "Since 1880 the theme of warfare has attracted the attention of practically every major novelist in the United States; the writing of a war novel has become a form of apprenticeship uniting authors whose prime interests lay in other areas." (Aichinger 106)

begins to question ultimate realities in a world that has become chaotically destructive and intensely vital--anything can happen in the extreme stress of the on-going life-and-death struggle. The characteristics of the real battlefield appear in our fictive accounts of the experience of war, and thus a similarly rich variety governs the imaginative renditions of combat. Moreover, warfare, in fact and fiction, has always evoked an equally wide variety of judgments from age to age, from one individual to another: love of heroic glory, grim acceptance of the destruction as a political necessity, passionate denunciation of all things military, savage satire, humour (good natured, scatological, absurdist, and black), patriotic fervour, elegiac sadness--there are as many different responses to warfare as there are to life itself.

Not surprisingly, then, the history of the critical responses to the *Iliad* illustrates, among other things, that a particular reader's understanding of the poem is shaped in large part by his personal vision of warfare. The great poet-critic Dryden, for example, who loved Homer and set out to translate the *Iliad*, delivered one of the harshest judgments ever made on the Iliadic warriors: "ungodly man-killers, whom we poets, when we flatter them, call heroes; a race of men who can never enjoy quiet in themselves, till they have taken it from all the world" (2:13). One hears in the remark the voice of the civilized Restoration man weary of the senseless slaughter in his own age and determined to seek hope in a new vision. Responses different from Dryden's led Alexander the Great to sleep with a copy of the *Iliad* under his pillow and Schliemann to christen his children by placing the text on their heads and reciting lengthy selections of Homeric verse. Pacifists echo Dryden, celebrators of the warrior virtues still maintain Alexander the Great's heroic dreams, and lovers of the sublime applaud Schliemann's ritual. No reader can objectively divorce his emotional attitude to warfare from his imaginative interaction with the text of Homer's poem. And to the extent that the reader of the *Iliad* brings to the epic an intelligent familiarity with real combat or with the literature of battle, his perceptions of the artistic treatment of warfare have already acquired a certain edge. For that reason, it makes perfect sense for a modern interpreter of the *Iliad* to introduce comparisons with, say, Shakespeare's *Henry V*, or Tolstoy's *War and Peace*, or Michael Herr's *Dispatches*, or Philip Caputo's *A Rumour of War*, or Michael Cimono's *Deer Hunter*, or, indeed, any other sensitive treatment of men in battle. For the general reader that sort of reference will often illuminate the complexities of Homer's poem much more quickly and accurately than will background historical facts. Conversely, the experience of reading the *Iliad* will almost certainly enrich the reader's critical understanding of other attitudes to war, including his own.

Even someone who has no detailed familiarity with the facts or the fictions of war will bring to the *Iliad* feelings and opinions about warfare. For the subject prompts an energetic response from almost everyone. There must be few topics, if any, about which people, regardless of their age, experience, education, and reading habits, are so instantly prepared to argue, confident of their own attitudes. War is an eternally popular topic of conversation and debate. The spokesmen for the peace groups will continue to argue that war is an inhumane institutionalized social power ritual that we should get rid of once and for all, the televisions will continue to show us colour footage of the front-line killings in Iran or Beirut, and the history books will bring home to us the incredible butchery of modern times. For all that, the subject continues to fascinate us. It is curious, too, that although war has been not only one of man's eternal occupations but also one of his favorite preoccupations, yet today our formal education never introduces the student to the subject. In his required reading he may run across the occasional war novel or war poem, and he may briefly consider an aspect of warfare as part of a course in philosophy, psychology, political science, or history, but that will normally be the extent of the university's or school's interest. We allocate places in the curriculum for the study of virtually all other subjects of importance to our culture; we leave the study of war as an independent discipline quite alone, except in the military institutes. Why this neglect in the face of the subject's popularity and obvious cultural importance, I do not know, unless the subject is somehow offensive to the liberal doctrines which have shaped the modern curriculum.[2]

If warfare has for thousands of years been a favorite subject for readers and writers, then without much doubt one of our most popular stories is the Trojan War, including its prelude and aftermath. From Homer's time to the present, no narrative can compete with this ancient tale for a hold on the popular imagination. The preparations for war, the events on the battlefield, and the adventures on the return home have provided an apparently endless inspiration to Western culture. Young children have always given the story pride of place, and artists from Homer's age, to imperial Rome, to Renaissance Europe, to nineteenth-century Germany, to the modern age have constantly mined our richest narrative treasure. We can attribute this phenomenon, in large part, to the cultural authority of Homer's and Virgil's epics, until quite recently an indispensable part of the education of the artist's public. Moreover,

---

2 Significant also are the conventions, the often misleading conventions, which have determined how historians have traditionally explained the conduct of men in combat. See, in this connection, the remarkably stimulating study of warfare by John Keegan in The Face of Battle. My understanding of Homer owes a great deal to Keegan's introductory discussion of the traditional interpretations of combat.

14

the wealth of incident in the saga has always offered a tempting variety of artistic possibilities: the fabulous mythological origins in the Judgment of Paris, the adventures of the rape-seduction of Helen, the grim heroic grandeur of the assembly of warriors, the pathos of Iphigeneia's fate, the bloody details of the battlefield culminating in the fiery destruction of Troy, the romantic ordeals of Odysseus, the tragic fate of Agamemnon, and the revenge of Orestes--these and the countless other narratives in the larger story of the war have made the Trojan expedition our most fecund artistic resource, rivalled only in this respect by the Old Testament. One could, after all, easily construct a very useful survey of Western culture based solely on the history of the artistic treatments of the Trojan War. Consequently, when we come to Homer's version of the story, most of us already possess some knowledge of the tale, vague or precise. To very few readers is the narrative wholly foreign.

II

Given this general familiarity with the story of the Trojan War, it can come as rather a surprise to discover just how much of the traditional tale Homer omits from the *Iliad*. For example, the epic makes no attempt to reacquaint us in any detail with the beginning or the end of the adventure. The poem occasionally makes a passing allusion to the origins of the war (for example at 3.46, 6.292, and 24.28), and the final destruction of Troy hangs over all the military exploits like a dark, vatic cloud. But the epic does not seize upon the narrative possibilities of the Judgment of Paris, the abduction of Helen, the sacrifice of Iphigeneia, the deceptions of Odysseus, Sinon's trick, the Trojan Horse, or the final attack on the city. None of these enthralling episodes (or many others contained in the legend) has a significant place in the narrative. We search the *Iliad* in vain for most of our favorite stories from the ancient tale. Homer's epic occupies a few weeks in the tenth year of the war; if we overlook the gaps, like the nine days' plague in Book One, the action in the *Iliad* covers only a few days, a very short time in a much longer experience, which the epic does not include. In other words, the *Iliad* does not present the Trojan War as a specific, discrete, and complete event, with a clear beginning, middle, and end. Unlike Herodotus and generations of story tellers ever since, Homer appears to have little interest in dwelling upon the long-term or short-term causes of the war, and, unlike Virgil, Homer omits the specific stratagems by which Troy fell, in spite of the fact that these events offer all sorts of opportunities for narrative variety, suspense, and excitement. Similarly, Homer leaves out many of the conventional possibilities of a war fiction. The *Iliad* contains none

15

of the normal unpredictable or romantic incidents common to tales of adventurous battle and very few specific comments on the tactics, manuevers, or practical details necessary for war. The *Iliad*, together with the *Odyssey*, may have become for the Greeks an encyclopedia of human conduct, but Plato's criticisms of that phenomenon in *The Republic* or Swift's satiric gibes in *Tale of a Tub* are sound, at least to the extent that there is a remarkable dearth of practical detail in the *Iliad*. Whatever Alexander the Great derived from the epic, it could not have provided much help to him as a manual of useful military field procedures.

These omissions have a very significant effect. They contribute to the narrative a sense that the war is not so much a particular experience with its unique shape and character (like, say, the Burmese or Italian campaigns in World War II), but something more general, universal, and permanent. By paying virtually no attention to the detailed chronology of the conflict from the beginning to the end, by leaving the war open ended, and by focusing on a very short, concentrated period of time, a very small part of a much longer event, Homer develops the sense that these battles, or ones just like them, have been going on and will go on for a long, long time, almost indefinitely. The conflicts are not discrete, unique episodes in the lives of the heroes, extraordinary events which they will someday put behind them when the campaign ends; these battles are their lives--past, present, and future. Of course, like Homer's original audience and all later readers of the *Iliad*, we know the end of the story, and the event is prophesied several times. But the epic does not complete the tale nor even provide much assurance that the fighting will ever cease. By the end of the last book, one is left with the feeling that the next day the war will continue, as before, and the day after, and the day after that, and on and on. Just as it has had no clear beginning, so it will have no clear end. In a similar way, the lack of emphasis in the narrative on individual resourcefulness in tactics, strategy, or trickery (of the sort common in the *Odyssey*, for example, or in popular war fictions where a small group of comrades saves the world by ingenuity, luck, and deception) creates a sense that this war is an unvarying, all-powerful experience common to all men; it is not something which the individual can, through his particular efforts, in any fundamental way alter. He cannot by superior wit affect the outcome, because the war is bigger and more enduring than anyone who fights in it. Homer, in other words, endows the war with a curiously fatalistic quality. Confronted with the inexhaustible prospect of perpetual combat, man seems trapped.

Our lot from youth to age
was given us by Zeus: danger and war

to wind upon the spindle of our years
until we die to the last man. (14.85)

To the modern reader the terms fate, fatalistic, and fatalism, always prominent in a discussion of Greek literature, may require clarification, for in common language these words have acquired some very loose connotations, and we no longer always use them specifically to describe metaphysical beliefs, our own modern orthodoxy being antithetical to talk of fate in the traditional sense. To assert that Homer presents a fatalistic vision of war is to claim that in the *Iliad* he pictures war as the fundamental condition of human existence, as man's fate. Man is born into a world governed by war. He did not choose this condition, and there is nothing he can do to change it. Just as his fathers and grandfathers had to deal with constant warfare, so does he, and so will his children and grandchildren. Human beings have no option in this matter. Whatever started the war and whatever will end it (if it ever does end) lie outside the realm of human control.

One should note here that this concept of fate carries with it no necessary sense of whether or not the preordained scheme of things is agreeable to man or not. One can, after all, have faith in a benevolent, best-of-all-possible-worlds fate or, alternatively, recognize the controller of human life as an unwelcome, malevolent, destructive creature (for example, a huge white whale). The crucial similarity is the insistence that man lives in a world governed by forces beyond individual or collective human control. Nor does the notion of fate necessarily carry with it a belief that man has no freedom, that everything he does is predestined. For if man cannot change the existing order of things, he can at least select the manner in which he will confront his fate. That, as we shall see later in this essay, gives to man the means of asserting his own human values in the face of an unalterable destiny. The terms fate and fatalistic, therefore, refer to a basic metaphysical assumption about the relationship between man and natural order, but they do not specify any particular response based on that assumption, for it is clear that human beings can accept the notion of fate and yet develop a number of alternative ways of organizing life appropriately.[3]

---

3 One of the most compelling reasons for undertaking a chronological study of Classical Greek literature is to follow the different ways in which, from one writer to the next, the responses to the realities of human fate change. Homer of the Iliad, Homer of the Odyssey, Herodotus, Aeschylus, Sophocles, Euripides, Thucydides, Aristophanes, and Plato--the central issue in each writer is the interaction between the unchanging order of the world and man's freedom to search for the significant response to his condition. The visions differ, but the quest for an ordered relationship remains the central imaginative impulse.

The narrative style of the *Iliad* continuously reinforces this vision of war as a fatalistic condition of human life. One important technique Homer uses to evoke this sense is a skilful double chronology. As we read the epic, we sense the passage of a certain length of time, a few months, and yet the sequence of events reaches us as a thick, crowded, rapid, linear series of intense moments occupying only a few days. The combination of the several lengthy interruptions (the nine days' plague, the twelve days' waiting for Zeus, the twelve days' maltreatment of Hektor's corpse, and the nine days' preparation for Hektor's funeral) with the rapidity of the action in between creates the effect of an intense, stressful, and yet almost interminably drawn-out experience. The relatively few days of fighting described in the epic are full of similar incidents, arranged in a dense and often repetitive order. Homer offers the reader no precise sense of the passing of time; we get the impression that bloody events follow hard upon each other's heels, but there is no detailed attention to the continuing chronology, so that we also get a sense that time plays no significant role in the fighting, because the combat will just go on and on. In the *Odyssey*, by contrast, we are well aware of the number of hours, days, months, or years Odysseus has spent on a particular adventure. In the *Iliad* the reader easily follows, and quickly gets caught up in, a crowded narrative in which he loses any accurate sense of the passing of time. The frequent flashbacks into the past or prophecies about the future, which almost invariably involve scenes of warriors in combat, further promote this feeling that warfare is the fact of life and that it follows no established pattern in which rest, reflection, or new tactics will provide some relief from the dense rush of daily experience in the killing zone.

The war in the *Iliad*, in other words, Homer describes in such a manner as to emphasise its constant, unremitting, unchanging fatal pressure upon all those participating in it. No matter what success or disappointment the warrior has experienced today, the situation he faces remains essentially the same. One mortal crisis follows closely upon the last demand of an imperious war, from which there is no let up, no escape. The individual episodes in the war, like the total war itself, do not have a separate, complete identity; they are part of a compact, on-going process which never stops, from which there is no respite until the final death which awaits each man. All truces are short and doomed to failure. Ironically, the only other significant pauses in the killing, extraordinary events, come when the warriors want to clear the dead away, to prepare the land to receive more bodies. And even then the remains of the corpses become useful material in keeping the war going: the living warriors can use the human residue in the construction of a defensive rampart (7.327 ff.). It is significant that the end of any particular book in the

18

Iliad does not usually signal the conclusion of a completed action, for the next book takes up the narrative immediately, right where the last one left off. Even sleep provides no relief from the constant presence of the war. Book Nine, for example, ends with an image of repose:

> *When they had spilt their wine*
> *they all dispersed, each man to his own hut,*
> *and lying down they took the gift of sleep.* (9.712)

But the opening of Book Ten immediately contradicts any suggestion that, as the warriors rest, the war has temporarily receded. It works its unrelenting, fatal power on Agamemnon still.

> *but their high commander,*
> *Agamémnon, lay beyond sweet sleep*
> *and cast about in tumult of the mind.* (10.3)

Earlier in the poem, on an occasion when the king does fall asleep, he gets no rest from the war, for Zeus sends him a false dream of conquering the Trojans, a vision which rouses him to disastrous action (2.5 ff.). The way in which Homer thus cancels abruptly the apparent pause suggested at the end of a particular day or book reminds us constantly that this war never sleeps.

Effects such as those I describe above deny the narrative any characteristic rhythm in the warrior's engagement with the conflict, any sense that the war is a structure of separate incidents with a coherent overall shape and purpose. Whereas in the *Odyssey*, for example, the hero brings each adventure to a definite end, and then, often heavy at heart, eats his fill, sleeps deeply, and rises refreshed the next rosy-fingered dawn to begin another unique encounter on his journey home, in the *Iliad* the characters are locked into a never-ending struggle, which continues without any regular pause, refreshment, significant change, or renewal, and with no sense of an ultimate collective goal which would end the fighting or at least provide a sense of practical purpose. This feature of Homer's war can unsettle readers, especially those who do not sense or do not wish to accept the fatalistic quality of this vision of combat and who therefore want the war story to have a much more definite and complete shape. In Voltaire's *Candide*, for example, Pococurante echoes a familiar eighteenth-century objection to the *Iliad*:

> [Homer is] no special delight of mine. . . . I was once made to believe that I took pleasure in reading him; but that constant recital of fights which are all alike, those gods who are always interfering but never decisively, that Helen who is the cause of the war and then scarcely takes any part in the story, that Troy which is always under siege and never taken--all that bores me to tears. I have sometimes asked scholars if reading it bored them as much as it bores me; everyone who answered frankly told me the book dropped from his hands like

But this criticism rather misses the point. For Homer deliberately creates the sense of war as an interminable fatal condition. The Argives, we know, seek to capture Troy and will eventually do so, but the fighting will go on. For in the world of the *Iliad* the constant emotional and physical pressure of warfare defines every minute of the warrior's life, including his memories of the past and his ambitions for the future.

As one reads the *Iliad*, one's attention constantly focuses upon a particular event or series of related events, and yet one is always aware of a much larger picture. The specific dramatic confrontation Homer presents at any one moment belongs to a long history of such moments. The famous digressions, which have attracted so much unfavorable criticism, create the inescapable sense that war is the condition of existence. Flashbacks to earlier times illustrate repeatedly that the nature of human fate has not changed, that personal armed combat defines man's life. Phoinix's long story of Meleagros, Aineias's boasting about his ancestry, Andromakhe's tale of her family--these and similar departures from the immediate present evoke a sense that for Iliadic man there is no world apart from war. The particular events on the battlefield before Troy play themselves out against this background of eternal combat. Nestor's speeches, in particular, continually remind the reader that human life has always meant fighting on the battlefield. And his age indicates that so long as man can lift a weapon, he must face the daily realities of the killing zone, until he dies.[4]

> "*Agamémnon, I too could wish I were*
> *that man who killed the great Ereuthalíôn.*
> *But the immortal gods have given men*
> *all things in season. Once my youth, my manhood,*
> *now my age has come*
>
> > *No less for that*
>
> *I have my place among the charioteers*
> *to counsel and command them. Duties fit*
> *for elder men, these are. . . . " (4.318)*

In a similar manner, Homer's treatment of his characters emphasises the universal condition of warfare. The *Iliad* contains hundreds of different names, and we quickly recognize that in this war nations have assembled from all over the known world. The canvas is always very crowded. In fact, of course, most of the significant action involves only a relatively small group of major figures, and these appear in an or-

---

4 Thus, the notion that Nestor's reminiscences provide some "greater relief" to ease the monotony of the battle descriptions in my view is rather misplaced (Kirk, Songs 348).

ganized sequence of individual actions, so that we never lose contact with the central thrust of the narrative. The nine most important characters (Akhilleus, Agamemnon, Athena, Apollo, Telamonian Aias, Diomedes, Hektor, Patroklos, and Zeus) and their small supporting cast (Oilean Aias, Antilokhos, Ares, Aineias, Hera, Idomeneus, Menelaos, Meriones, Nestor, Odysseus, Paris, Poseidon, Priam, and Sarpedon) account for virtually every important incident in the poem, but we always see them in the midst of a huge international assembly of numberless gods and fighting men. From this all-inclusive, international group there is no escape.

Moreover, Homer's descriptions of the Akhaians and the Trojans gives to this war the impersonality of an omnipotent fatal presence governing all men. Apart from their different positions in the field, the Trojans and Akhaians are the same. They speak the same language, worship the same gods, live by the same heroic code, share the same style in rituals, prayers, burial customs, government, weapons, food, and art. Some warriors who oppose each other now belong to the same extended family and share common ancestors. They have entertained each other in the past, and their forefathers have fought as allies. Even many of the names are interchangeable. In Book Eight, for example, Agelaos is a Trojan warrior killed by Diomedes (8.257); soon afterwards, an Akhaian warrior of the same name is killed by Hektor (11.302).[5] Such a marked emphasis on the overwhelming similarities between the opposing forces contradicts any attempt to force onto the poem an important ethnic basis for the conflict and therefore adds weight to the impression that this war transcends the culture of any particular group participating in it.[6]

Indeed, throughout the *Iliad* we are reminded by the similarities between the opponents that this conflict does not originate in some rational economic, cultural, or religious quarrel. Even the treatment of Helen, a major character in the legend but a relatively unimportant character in the epic, provides no sufficient explanation for what is going on. If the abduction counts at all, it strikes us as a very minor pretext for doing what

5 Some other names used in this fashion are Antiphos, Adrestos, Alastor, Amphimakhos, Areilukos, Medon, Noemon, Orestes, Peisandros, and Tlepolemos.

6 For this reason, I find it difficult to accept an analysis of the war which insists upon significant qualitative differences between the opponents. For example, Lessing's comment in Laokoon strikes me as an inappropriate distortion of the evidence in the text: "If Homer lets the Trojans march into battle with wild cries, the Greeks on the other hand in determined silence, critics and commentators have not been slow to note that the poet intended by this to describe the former as barbarians, but the latter as civilized people" (quoted in Wilkinson and Willoughby 294). For obvious reasons, the attempt to see in the poem important cultural differences between the Akhaians and the Trojans often goes hand in hand with a desire to moralize the war, that is, to turn it into a contest between sinners and justified punishers. Chapter 7 of this essay discusses other examples of this critical tendency.

21

the men do all the time anyway. The one suggestion that the Trojans might want to debate the issue immediately evaporates (7.345 ff.); Priam does not take the notion seriously. He treats Antenor's point that they should give Helen back a good deal more politely than Odysseus does Thersites' wish to go home, but Priam's response has the same effect: the war continues as before. Consequently, we cannot easily grasp at first why these two armies are so keen on killing each other. For the notion that war is an impersonal fatal condition in which man is forever caught presents a view of the undertaking quite foreign to the modern reader. Whatever our opinions about war, we are used to thinking of it in terms of rational human objectives. The wars we are familiar with occur as specific historical events, with human causes, planned battles, human error, success, a more-or-less coherent sequence of strategic decisions and actions, and a conclusion. However chaotic the conduct of war may be and however unexpected the outcome, most of us think of it as something which we to some extent control, perhaps imperfectly and often unwisely, but control nevertheless. We search the *Iliad* in vain for such familiar criteria of war.

When someone refers to the "strangeness" of the *Iliad* or when, for example, Rieu pays tribute to the terror in the poem (vii), he is surely referring more than anything else to the dislocation the reader experiences with this vision of warfare. The brutality of war in the *Iliad*--and no writer or film-maker depicts more graphically than Homer what goes on in hand-to-hand combat--we are familiar with, but the fatalistic vision of war contradicts the modern liberal-progressive tradition which shapes the way most of us think and argue about the subject. The point is not that many of us, especially young adults, are fervent pacifists instantly disillusioned by the military ethic, although that may be part of it, but that we have inherited a faith in man's ability to shape his own destiny. For us, evils like war are socio-political or psychological problems, created by man and capable of resolution through human effort. Even those modern war fictions which present the dreadful carnage in full screen technicolour images and Dolby sound usually insist upon the human responsibility for the event, and television coverage of front-line atrocities customarily involves some rational analysis of human causes, aims, and responsibilities. Inasmuch as these modern investigations of war can be said to have a moral purpose, they usually strive to foster in us the awareness that we can and should do something to avoid or minimize the bloodshed. Thus, the fatalism in the *Iliad* can be ominous.

Perhaps it is not so surprising, then, that a first experience of the *Iliad* often produces the snap judgment that Homer's characters are nothing more than psychopaths in love with butchery and that, therefore, the poem is a hymn to martial madness. That reaction offers an obvious defense against exploring Homer's vision any further. Even thoughtful and informed critics of the *Iliad* can demonstrate an unwillingness to accept the full imaginative implications of this fatalistic picture of war. The history of Homeric criticism reveals an enduring desire on the part of many interpreters to fit the war into a traditional moral framework, that is, to transform the warfare in the *Iliad* from a universal, fatal condition into a specific event with a coherent rational purpose, punishment for Trojan crimes. The effect of such a view of the poem, of course, is to adapt Homer's vision to something much more familiar (and therefore less imaginatively unsettling) to us. However, it seems to me--and this point lies at the very heart of this essay--that Homer's emphasis throughout the poem is quite the opposite, for he offers us no clear cultural or moral distinctions between the opponents and insists upon their common identity as human beings rather than on any qualitative differences between them.

III

Before we read very much of the *Iliad*, we have to acknowledge that the vision of war in this poem has at least two apparently contradictory qualities: on the one hand, it evokes an inspiring sense of beauty, courage, and individual glory; on the other, it insists upon the extreme brutality and inhumanity of individual and mass butchery. To seize upon only one part of Homer's vision, or to inflate one side of this duality at the expense of the other, is seriously to misrepresent the ironic tension at the heart of the epic. For example, in Lewis Milestone's film *All Quiet on the Western Front*, the German schoolteacher, one of the villains of the piece, fills the young boys with patriotic fervour for military glory in the service of the fatherland, invoking the classical authority of the first words of the *Iliad* to reinforce his pedagogical message, which the film then sets out to dismantle. No doubt, the scene accurately reflects the construction once put upon the *Iliad* by many teachers, and the film offers a justly famous indictment of such unthinking patriotic militarism. But we should not confuse the teacher and his use of the *Iliad* here with an accurate understanding of the poem. In the same way, we must resist too quickly seeing in Homer's emphasis upon the dreadful slaughter an overt anti-war message.[7] For at the heart of the poem is an equally poised balance between two conflicting aspects of the central enterprise.

7 See, for example, the very well-known pacifist reading of the Iliad by Simone Weil. In the introduction to his Penguin translation, E. V. Rieu suggests that Homer's main purpose is "not to glorify war (though it admits its fascination) but to emphasize its tragic futility" (xviii).

On one side, Homer's vision continually holds before us the graphic details of death in single combat. Unlike many traditional apologists for militarism, the "See the noble defenders of our native land sleeping peacefully upon the fields of honour" school of war poets, Homer never takes convenient refuge from the slaughter in euphemism or gentle elegiac fuzziness.

> *With the bone*
> *itself, the vicious stone crushed both leg tendons*
> *utterly, and the tall man tumbled down*
> *into the dust, flinging his arms out wide*
> *to his companions, panting his life away;*
> *but on the run the man who hit him, Peiros,*
> *came with a spear to gash him by the navel.*
> *His bowels were spilled, and darkness veiled his eyes. (4.521)*

> *At this he made his cast,*
> *his weapon being guided by Athêna*
> *to cleave Pándaros' nose beside the eye*
> *and shatter his white teeth: his tongue*
> *the brazen spearhead severed, tip from root,*
> *then plowing on came out beneath his chin.*
> *He toppled from the car, and all his armor*
> *clanged on him, shimmering. The horses*
> *quivered and shied away; but life and spirit*
> *ebbed from the broken man, and he lay still. (5.290)*

> *Pênéleos drove his spearhead*
> *into the eye-socket underneath the brow,*
> *thrusting the eyeball out. The spearhead ran*
> *straight through the socket and the skull behind,*
> *and throwing out both hands he sat down backward.*
> *Pênéleos, drawing his long sword, chopped through*
> *the nape and set the severed helmeted head*
> *and trunk apart upon the field. The spear*
> *remained in the eye-socket. (14.493)*

> *Idómeneus thrust hard at Erymas' mouth*
> *with his hard bronze. The spearhead passed on through*
> *beneath his brain and split the white brain-pan.*
> *His teeth were dashed out, blood filled both his eyes,*
> *and from his mouth and nostrils as he gaped*
> *he spurted blood. Death's cloud enveloped him. (16.345)*

One need not multiply these examples. They make the point sufficiently clear. Homer neither spares us nor sensationalizes the details. The descriptions have a clinical precision ("into the eye-socket underneath the brow") and an almost cinematic emphasis on the stage-by-stage progress of the deadly weapon through the living flesh and bone in a series of vivid stills: entry, stage one, stage two, exit from the body, final agony, death. The style forces the reader to witness, moment by moment, exactly what this battle involves: the destructive, brutal, ugly pain and waste. One finds here no easy emphasis on military glory.

Two other features of Homer's descriptions of the deaths in the killing zone make them all the more eloquent images of the inhumanity of war. First, almost inevitably, the warriors, even those who are not major figures, are introduced to us before they die. Each has a name, often a family identity, with parents, wife, and children, and a distant homeland. This particular death, even among so many, Homer constantly reminds us, involves a unique human being. We thus have no emotional escape from the killing in the comforting anonymity of the victim, of the sort that we regularly find in a less grim vision, like the *Odyssey*, where almost all of those who die en route, though comrades of Odysseus, remain strangers to us. There the savage reality of violent death is usually kept at a safe distance, so that we can focus on the comic energies of the hero. In the *Iliad*, the identification of the warrior, however brief, brings him to life as an individual who matters. Second, Homer typically concludes a description of death with a reminder that what was once, a few moments ago, a gloriously vital human being is now forever gone, transformed into inert meat. Death, the final rest, contains no entry to another world; no Paradise, Valhalla, Elysian Fields, or Heaven awaits these warriors. The loss of human life is absolute, for death, the "black nightmare," extinguishes human existence utterly. The appearance of the ghost of Patroklos confirms this impression, for it brings Akhilleus and the reader a sense of the overwhelming meaninglessness of death. [8] Upright the soldier may express beauty, courage, and passion. On the ground he is only fit for scavenging wild animals. The fallen soldier's armour echoes because it is now empty, because the life has forever gone from it; nothing remains but an empty metal shell. And the fight over the corpse matters often because the warriors value the metal now that the man has gone. Thus, the well-known laconic final phrases (darkness veiling the eyes, teeth grinding in the dust, bodies left as food for carrion) resonate through the entire poem as a recurring, cryptic litany, insisting upon the

8 In this regard, see N. J. Richardson: "as one might have expected, the belief in punishment in the underworld may have already been a popular one in Homer's time, as it certainly was later, but the poet has chosen not to give it any prominence. The Iliad in particular presents a very austere picture of the after-life as a total contrast with life on earth, and neither rewards nor punishments would have suited the poet's bleak conception of death as the common end for all men alike, whether good or bad, humble or great" (54).

grim finality of death. For us the expression "bit the dust" may have become trite, a common euphemism hiding an unpleasant reality or even nowadays a mindless slogan for the triumphant fans at a sporting event. In the *Iliad* the expression has all the vivid anatomical reality and emotional shock of the final agonizing death throes. For Homer never spares us the vivid reality of death, the final, brutal end of vital individual existence.

But in the *Iliad* battle has at the same time another dimension. It also prompts the noblest and most beautiful human conduct. In the ranks of the warriors, the individual realizes his potential for an extraordinary manifestation of human values. The stress of combat challenges the heroic man to declare himself, to stand up bravely in the face of mortal danger, to stare unwaveringly at fate, and to meet it on his own terms. Later on in this essay (in Chapter 4) we shall be examining in greater detail the conduct of the Iliadic warrior; suffice it to say here that Homer repeatedly pays tribute to the powerful exultation, the passionate joy, and the wonderful courage which accompany the man who is prepared to declare himself and to risk his life in response to the "fiery ardor for the battle-test that brings honor to men" (4.223). Not by accident does Athena, the goddess of wisdom, who, we may recall, sprung to life fully armed, also function as a presiding deity of battle, who summons from soldiers the most deeply felt sense of beauty and joy in life itself.

> *So down the ranks that dazzling goddess went*
> *to stir the attack, and each man in his heart*
> *grew strong to fight and never quit the mêlée,*
> *for at her passage war itself became*
> *lovelier than return, lovelier than sailing*
> *in the decked ships to their own native land. (2.450)*

In such passages Homer evokes a sense of how, by the most extraordinary of ironies, war releases essential creative instincts. It heightens man's sense of life, his joy in his humanness, his sense of beauty in the world, and his love and respect for his fellow man, including, by the greatest paradox of all, even his enemy. With this aspect of Homer's picture of war, many modern readers may have some difficulty. But if we are to appreciate the poem fully, we cannot cope with the problems this may pose for us by denying its importance or by dismissing it as a "primitive" cultural response appropriate only to ancient warrior societies or to deranged militarists, for the literature of modern battle reminds us that Athena has not yet quit the front lines.

But once it was actually going on, things were different. You were just like everyone else, you could no more blink than spit. It came back the same way every time, dreaded and welcome, balls and bowels turning over together, your senses working like strobes, free-falling all the way down to the essences and then flying out again in a rush to focus, like the first strong twinge of tripping after an infusion of psilocybin, reaching in at the point of calm and springing all the joy and dread every known, ever known by everyone who ever lived, un-utterable in its speeding brilliance. Touching all the edges and then passing, as though it had been controlled from outside, by a god or by the moon (Herr 143).

Thus, at the heart of the *Iliad* we have the central ironic tension, the dual nature of warfare. It exalts men and impartially destroys them; it releases joyous passion and extinguishes life forever; it realizes many of the supreme human virtues and utterly annihilates those who best embody those virtues. War includes Athena the beautiful, the "Hope of Soldiers," and Ares the brutal, the "bane of all mankind, crusted with blood, breacher of city walls," the divine siblings presiding over the battlefield, inextricably and permanently linked together.

War devours differences and disparities, shows no respect for the unique. Call him Achilles or Hector, the conqueror is like all conquerors, and the conquered like all the conquered. Homer does not spare us this sight. But at the same time he sees warlike emulation as the fountainhead of creative effort, as the spring of individual energy and of the manly virtues in the community. (Bespaloff 48)

IV

The long introduction to the first engagement between the Akhaians and the Trojans in Book Four, our first experience of group combat in the epic, establishes clearly the irony characteristic of Homer's vision. The preparation for the coming battle draws our attention to the passionate individuality of these warriors, who define their splendid existence by their participation in destructive combat.

> *In that hour*
> *no one could have perceived in Agamémnon*
> *a moment's torpor or malingering, but fiery*
> *ardor for the battle-test that brings*
> *honor to men. (4.223)*

The Akhaian leader tours the lines, calling attention to each of the great warrior chiefs: Idomeneus, Telamonian Aias, Oilean Aias, Nestor, Odysseus, Diomedes, Sthenelos. Each of them appears before us in turn declaring his fierce pride, courage, and strength. Then, the whole mass of armed men gathers together under the irresistible and beautiful force of war.

> *As down upon a shore of echoing surf*
> *big waves may run under a freshening west wind,*

looming first on the open sea, and riding
shoreward to fall on sand in foam and roar,
around all promontories crested surges
making a briny spume inshore--so now
formations of Danááns rose and moved
relentlessly toward combat. Every captain
called to his own. The troops were mainly silent;
you could not have believed so great a host
with warcries in its heart was coming on
in silence, docile to its officers--
and round about upon the soldiers shone
the figured armor buckled on for war. (4.422)

The moment evokes the awe-inspiring power and sublime beauty and threat of war, that paradoxical combination of fascination, loveliness, and danger conveyed, for example, in the later images of fire and in the connotations of the noun-verb *glitter*, justifiably a favorite word with translators of Homer's battle scenes.

As soon as the fighting starts, however, our response shifts, for the details force our attention onto how the demands of mortal combat change the brilliant, heroic control evident in the coming-on for battle into something increasingly savage and desperate. The combatants start "going for one another like wolves, like wolves whirling upon each other, man to man" (4.471). The immediate juxtaposition here of man and wolves brings out the ironic destructiveness of the battle, for the proud, superbly controlled heroic individual warriors have now become frantic, whirling, destructive beasts. The final image of Book Four, however, qualifies this sense and adds another dimension to our response. We follow the deaths of Diores Amarungkeides and then the immediate retribution on his slayer, Peiros Imbrasides (4.517 ff.). Death for death. Finally we see the effects of the endeavour which began only a few moments before with the pictures of the noble warriors getting ready: "throngs of Trojans and Akhaians, prone in the dust, were strewn beside each other" (4.543). From the proud individual leaders determined to establish their personal glory in hand-to-hand combat against the enemy we have come to the picture of the equal anonymity of death: a heap of indistinguishable Trojan and Akhaian corpses, food for carrion in the indifferent dust.

The fighting in Homer's poem involves a good deal more than this introduction in Book Four, of course, as we discover in the opening of Book Five, but the first description of a normal encounter acquaints the reader with some of the complex ambiguities of the experience. The battle emphasises individuality, order, and human worth and degrades and destroys what it makes possible. Homer's irony here is not loaded against one side of the duality. The pathetic slaughter does not under-cut the values of heroic individualism, as it does, for example, in Wilfred Owen's poetry. Nor does the emphasis on military glory try to justify the terrible killing, as does the "blood is the god of war's rich livery" rhetoric of Marlowe. The irony, like the war itself, is impersonal, detached. The warfare is not, in any conventional sense, good or bad; it just is what it is, an eternally fated contradiction:

> *in one same air elation and agony*
> *of men destroying and destroyed, and earth*
> *astream with blood. (4.450)*

CHAPTER 3

War, Nature, and the Gods

"War is the father of all and the king of all; and some he has made gods and some men, some bond and some free." (Herakleitos, Fragment 44)

I

The full weight of Homer's ironic vision of war as the fatal condition of human life begins to make itself felt in the opening pages of the *Iliad* when we sense that the experience in the front line of battle is not an isolated phenomenon but an integral part of nature and, beyond that, of the metaphysical order of the universe. For although Homer's depictions of war always highlight particular individual human beings in combat, nevertheless this war is never merely human. It takes place in a wider setting that includes not just the different groups of individual warriors, often with friends and family absent in distant places, but also the natural and the divine structure of the world. The human conflict, therefore, remains always an essential part of an all-inclusive natural and cosmic drama. War does not confine itself to the clashes between the Trojans and the Akhaians; warring forces also constantly strive against each other in the natural world, and irrational oppositions govern the heavenly order of things. This extension of the ambiguities of war into every corner of experience becomes most evident in the two features of the poem I consider in this chapter: the descriptions of nature and the portrayal of the gods.

The most obvious method Homer constantly employs to place the particular physical human encounters within the context of a wider natural strife is the famous Homeric simile, that formal comparison over several lines, in which the two objects brought together in the comparison are described in considerable detail. Characteristically, this trope directly links the actions of the men on the battlefield with common natural phenomena.

31

As in dark forests, measureless along
the crests of hills, a conflagration soars,
and the bright bed of fire glows for miles,
now fiery lights from this great host in bronze
played on the earth and flashed high into heaven.

And as migrating birds, nation by nation,
wild geese and arrow-throated cranes and swans,
over Asïa's meadowland and marshes
around the streams of Kaystrios, with giant
flight and glorying wings keep beating down
in tumult on that verdant land
that echoes to their pinions, even so,
nation by nation, from the ships and huts,
this host debouched upon Skamánder plain.
With noise like thunder pent in earth
under their trampling, under the horses' hooves,
they filled the flowering land beside Skamánder,
as countless as the leaves and blades of spring.
So, too, like clouds of buzzing, fevered flies
that swarm about a cattle stall in summer
when pails are splashed with milk: so restlessly
by thousands moved the fighters of Akhaia
over the plain, lusting to rend the Trojans. (2.455)

The normal structure of the simile, of which the above quote is a typical example, holds up an extended comparison in which an image of the antagonistic forces of nature, especially those of the sea against the shore, fire in the forests or the fields, wind on the crops, or beasts of prey attacking domestic livestock or man, transfers the attributes of natural strife and destruction onto the soldiers ("Just as these opposing forces of nature, so these men at war"). In the process, the comparison insists simply and directly upon the similarity between natural events and the urge to human combat. Often the simile reinforces the central paradox of war, for the forces of nature, like fire and storm, are simultaneously enticing, often fiercely beautiful, yet also irresistibly destructive. The shift in verb tenses, too, emphasises the union of the past behaviour of the warriors and the present dynamics of nature: just as the forces of nature always act in this way, so those soldiers fought then. Moreover, the wide range of natural and geographical references in the similes (to birds, distant lands, rivers, mountains, farms, forests, and so on) repeatedly links the particular experience in this continuing human battle to the ceaseless universal strife which has always governed natural events. The urge to conflict pushes the soldiers on with a power as deeply rooted as the migrating instincts of the birds, as common as the spring growth of the leaves, and as inevitable and familiar as the feeding of flies. In the great spectrum of timeless natural phenomena, from the most aristocratic and powerful lords of the air to the buzzing pests of the stall, war occupies a place, and its presence in all the eternal rhythms of nature underscores its impersonal omnipotence, its irrefutable rightness. The epic similes in the *Iliad* keep insisting that war springs from the very same sources as those events which have always made the world function the way it does. Warfare is thus not a human aberration but an integral part of the irresistible, eternal, and mysterious natural order of things.

The aptness of the comparison between natural and human forces emerges also in the energy which the Homeric simile typically gathers. For each simile characteristically presents a comparison developed over many lines, so that as the details accumulate, the momentum in the verse gathers force, without significant pause. The formal introduction to the comparison interrupts the narrative action, holding it up momentarily against a backdrop of universal and timeless nature, and then, as the simile develops, the verse gathers momentum and finally delivers the full energy of the unwinding sentence onto the key words, usually verbs denoting action. In the passage quoted above, for example, the extended multiple comparisons continue over many lines; the energy in the verse increases and finally brings its full accumulated weight to bear on the word describing the power with which the army moved, "debouched," an odd word, but its sound value helps one to appreciate why the translator has chosen it. The movement in the verse continues into another comparison, and, once again, the accumulating momentum greatly heightens the impact of the words which direct the comparison onto the men at war ("restlessly," "moved," "lusting to rend"). We know what these words denote, of course, but by the time we reach the line, the simile invests the words with a range of natural reference and a stored-up power which enable us more fully to grasp the emotional significance of the scene. This use of an extended simile to create in the movement of a verse paragraph the feeling of irresistible emotional power is familiar enough to readers of Milton and Wordsworth. In Homer's epic style, which these poets were, in part, emulating, the technique works again and again to reinforce our sense that the warfare is not an unnatural human mistake but a normal response to the eternal and irresistible powers of nature.

All similes, however, contain in their structure a latent irony. For while they insist upon the similarities between two apparently unrelated things, they also implicitly call attention to the differences. The poetic effects of a simile depend upon the appropriate relationship between the two contradictory tendencies of any comparison. When we describe a simile as unsuccessful, for example, we usually dismiss it either because the similarity is too far-fetched and strained, that is, because the differences overwhelm any illuminating similarities, or because the similarity is so obvious, with no sense of difference at work, that the trope has become emotionally empty and trite, a cliche. Some of the subtlest effects in poetry depend upon the intricate double nature of the comparison. A simple illustration of this duality is Homer's most famous metaphor, "the winedark sea." The comparison offers us immediately a sense of the rich attractiveness of the ocean, the fascination with the hidden emotional powers of nature. For the sea, like dark wine, benefits man, tempts him, intoxicates him, and can overpower the unwary. On the other hand, the sea in many important ways is quite unlike wine. The sea can be a savage opponent; it often unexpectedly and irresistibly destroys the man who follows his urge to experience it. The killer sea is not, like wine, a central part of convivial feasts or libations to the powerful gods. Wine is produced by human skill and has become an essential part of peaceful civilized life. The sea, by contrast, follows its own whims and cannot be made a permanent and predictable part of anyone's peaceful social existence; its eternally bitter vintage arises from and works by some mysterious, ambiguous power uncontrolled by man. The complex paradox in the apparently simple metaphor simultaneously insists upon both the similarity and the difference.

In the same way, the successful Homeric simile often presents a complex process in which the vivid image both places the war in a universal natural context and yet also reminds the reader that the experience of battle denies certain vital human alternatives.

> *Think of two men contending over boundary stones,*
> *each with his measuring rod, in the common field,*
> *in a narrow place, disputing what is fair:*
> *so here the parapet divided these.... (12.421)*

> *But at the hour*
> *a woodsman takes his lunch in a cool grove*
> *of mountain pines, when he has grown arm-weary*
> *chopping tall timber down, and, sick of labor,*
> *longs for refreshment--at that height of noon*
> *Danáäns calling fiercely back and forth*
> *broke the Trojan line. (11.86)*

> *As north wind in late summer*
> *quickly dries an orchard freshly watered,*
> *to the pleasure of the gardener, just so*
> *the whole reach of the plain grew dry, as fire*
> *burned the corpses. (21.346)*

Remarkable in these examples, selected at random, as in many of the similes from the *Iliad*, is the way in which the comparison works both ways. We see the point of the similarity, but the differences also introduce a certain ironic resonance. For surveyors, woodsmen, and the north wind in summer blowing through an orchard all suggest human possibilities other than battle, a civilization based on an order and creative effort different from the life of the front-line warrior. Thus, we discover in the comparisons the limitations of warfare, the range of human possibilities which the activity necessarily leaves out. While the similes often place the destructive results of battle in the midst of a universal natural order, they also indicate repeatedly that the vision of war is a constricted, narrow view of human life, for the ironic implications of the comparison reveal how war inevitably denies common civilized options. Warriors in the *Iliad* display all the irrational, unpredictable ferocity of the north wind; but they bring no pleasure to gardeners, whose creative desires encourage useful, peaceful growth of living things. Soldiers, we know from what we read in the epic, water the earth with human blood, and their passionate creative energies, though natural and frequently beautiful, have no room for horticulture. Fields of glory, Homer's similes remind us, can also be cattle pasture. But armies drive the cattle from the fields and bury human beings beneath the earth. Spears have obvious similarities to measuring rods, but the surveyor's life differs fundamentally from the spearman's. And while chopping down opponents in battle has some clear metaphorical connections to chopping down mighty trees, the woodsman has a peaceful creative purpose central to home, trade, and art; moreover, his victims are not living fellow men. In this way, the similes constantly present to us different forms of civilized creativity, more prosaic and peaceful alternatives, which the warrior, by the nature of his life, cannot see, cannot include in his response to the natural forces which drive him to battle, cannot admit into his vision of what stamps human life with worthy purpose. Sometimes the effects of this reminder of a world beyond the war can quite startle the reader.

> *Comparable to the throes*
> *a writhing woman suffers in hard labor*
> *sent by the goddesses of Travail, Hêra's*
> *daughters, Twisters, mistresses of pangs,*
> *the anguish throbbed in Agamémnon now. (11.269)*

Considering that Agamemnon's pain comes from a wound he has suffered while gloriously exterminating a whole series of young men in battle, we see the ironic implications of Homer's comparison. Whatever war gives birth to, the price includes the wholesale destruction of human life.

The double nature of the Homeric simile does not work to lessen the importance or the established value of either side of the comparison. We do not, that is, face any satiric suggestion that the life outside the battlefield is a realistic and worthy alternative which the warrior, if he would only abandon his immoral conduct, should obviously prefer. The similes rather evoke continually the feeling that the war in the *Iliad* creates a human existence which is both extraordinarily passionate, destructive, beautiful, and natural, and at the same time very confining. In his similes Homer emphasises war's rightful place in nature and the severe limitations it imposes on human nature. In recognizing one, we cannot escape an awareness of the other. As a result, the style repeatedly introduces into our response to the war an ironic complexity that we cannot easily sum up.

> *Then*
> *in his turn Meneláos made his lunge,*
> *calling on Zeus. The spearhead pierced the young man's*
> *throat at the pit as he was falling back,*
> *and Meneláos with his heavy grip*
> *drove it on, straight through his tender neck.*
> *He thudded down, his gear clanged on his body,*
> *and blood bathed his long hair, fair as the Graces',*
> *braided, pinched by twists of silver and gold.*
> *Think how a man might tend a comely shoot*
> *of olive in a lonely place, well-watered,*
> *so that it flourished, being blown upon*
> *by all winds, putting out silvery green leaves,*
> *till suddenly a great wind in a storm*
> *uprooted it and cast it down: so beautiful*
> *had been the son of Pánthoös, Euphórbos,*
> *when Meneláos killed him and bent over*
> *to take his gear.*
> *And as a mountain lion*
> *cuts out a yearling from a grazing herd. . . . (17.45)*

The power, ferocity, glory, waste, butchery, pain--all are inherently part of the one awesome destiny uniting the destroyer and the destroyed. The mysterious and divine fertility of nature, the source of life, energy, joy, and beauty, brings forth all things, including, paradoxically, the forces of human destruction and destructiveness. From nature itself issue those fatal powers which return men "motionless to the life-bestowing earth" (3.244).

II

The warfare in the *Iliad*, however, is considerably more than part of the natural and human world--it belongs also in the metaphysical order of the cosmos, the divine structure according to which everything behaves the way it does. The very opening lines of the poem at once indicate the intimate connections between the story Homer has set out to tell and the gods who rule all.

> *Anger be now your song, immortal one,*
> *Akhilleus' anger, doomed and ruinous,*
> *that caused the Akhaians loss on bitter loss*
> *and crowded brave souls into the undergloom,*
> *leaving so many dead men--carrion*
> *for dogs and birds; and the will of Zeus was done. (1.1)*

This invocation leads directly to the religious paradox at the heart of the poem. The epic, we are told, will describe the horrible, inhuman process by which living beings, brave souls, are destroyed in war, doomed in great numbers to become rotting meat for scavenging animals--and all according the will of Zeus. The structure of the sentence, which leaves the mention of Zeus until after the strong language describing mortal disaster, so that the notion that all these horrible events take place according to his will reaches us almost as a casual afterthought, emphasises the sudden shock of the announcement. The terrible waste of human life proceeds from divine desires. The opening juxtaposition of death in battle and the emotions of the gods introduces the reader to the idea that all the details in the story which follows, even the most inhumane, rightfully belong in the metaphysical order of the universe and proceed from the gods. We know none of the particulars yet, but we recognize that the gods are going to be an inextricable, formative part of this bloody war.

The question which follows a few lines after the opening invocation, "Among the gods, who brought this quarrel on?" (1.8), defines precisely the strangeness in the vision we are being introduced to. For what essentially determines the shape of a belief is not the answers it provides, important as these may be, but the questions human beings ask. The interrogatives themselves necessarily indicate the form the answer will take. And significantly, the opening lines of the *Iliad* set up for us the main theme of the poem and immediately indicate in the subsequent question where the explanation for this extraordinary tale must lie. The question implies clearly that the crisis must have a cosmic origin in the wishes of a particular god. Human actions have no ultimate bearing on

37

the matter. The poem does not even pause momentarily to consider the possibility that the origin might be problematic and need careful exploration before a firm answer is given. The narrator confidently asserts in the question that the responsibility obviously rests with one of the gods. That cause being self-evident, men should reflect on which god behaves in this way and how they can discover some method to appease his ire. We do not have to wait long to discover the motive.

> Agamémnon
> angered him, so he made a burning wind
> of plague rise in the army: rank and file
> sickened and died for the ill their chief had done
> in despising a man of prayer. (1.11)

A reader who cherishes a faith in a benevolent or reasonable deity will not find this first image of divine conduct particularly reassuring, especially when he learns of the details of the insult to the priest and the disproportionately severe general slaughter wrecked by Apollo, nine days of "transfixing pain" and death to satisfy the passionate anger of a god. The narrative, we should note, does not suggest that Apollo acts here the part of some legalistic Jehovah, punishing human beings for transgressing established holy commandments, nor is he trying to teach men any clear lesson in proper behaviour. The god destroys hundreds of animals and men because his irrational rage over an insult drives him to it. His conduct makes the reader confront the most obviously puzzling aspect of the gods in the *Iliad*, their irrational passion and the totally destructive power they characteristically unleash to sate their own emotional appetites. In case we fail to sense just how much Apollo follows his own immediate feelings, the epic shows us that by the end of Book One he has ceased even to care about the destruction he has caused and the quarrel he has initiated. Instead he sits contentedly among his peers playing music (1.603).

Throughout the *Iliad* we see the gods acting, as Apollo does here, according to nothing we can recognize as a rational, legal, humanistic, or ethical principle. They base their actions on passion, on irrational responses similar to the feelings that occur in human life, although the effects are enormously different in degree, of course. Moreover, the reader clearly sees very quickly that the gods are inextricably bound up with the human fighting; indeed, the origin and the conduct of the war would be inconceivable without the constant interference of the Olympian deities. For this reason, no attempt to understand Homer's vision of warfare can afford to ignore or to minimize the importance of these gods. The Iliadic warriors recognize that the divine wills shape everything that happens to them, good and bad. Consequently, if we wish to interpret the vision of experience developed for us in the *Iliad*, we must

38

necessarily come to grips with a system of belief quite different from our own. The full irony of Homer's war one can only understand by exploring the details of the metaphysical order which creates and sustains it.[1]

We might begin by recognizing the importance of the physical shapes of the gods and their inter-relationships in a large family. For the divine order in the *Iliad* has a symbolic form which immediately makes the immortal deities emotionally intelligible to their human subjects. Not only do the gods appear as sharply etched individual men and women, with all the characteristics of powerful, often peevish rulers, but they exist together in a loosely knit family and display all the very familiar emotional actions of human beings in such a situation: they both love and hate members of the clan; they bicker constantly, for reasons which are often not entirely clear, and then later make up; they trick each other and then establish alliances; they tease, insult, abuse, and respect each other; they argue about areas of authority, family friends, honour, and a host of other problems quite familiar to anyone who has had any experience of life in an extended family. The reader's first lengthy glimpse of the assembly of gods is very revealing.

> *Abruptly*
> *and with oblique intent to ruffle Hêra,*
> *Zeus in cutting tones remarked.... (4.5)*

> *At this proposal, Hêra and Athêna*
> *murmured rebelliously. These two together*
> *sat making mischief for the men of Troy,*
> *and though she held her tongue, a sullen anger*
> *filled Athêna against her father. Hêra*
> *could not contain her own vexation.... (4.20)*

> *Coldly annoyed,*
> *the Lord Zeus, who drives the clouds of heaven,*
> *answered.... (4.30)*

We might almost be watching an installment of *Dallas* or *Dynasty*. The comparison is not wholly trivial; it reminds us that one of the most accessible symbols in all popular fiction is the family, especially the family quarrel, for it provides an immediate contact with the common experiences in the daily life of the artist's audience. Virtually everyone fighting the Trojan War or reading Homer's epic knows something about authoritarian fathers, jealous sisters, bickering mothers, and petty fami-

---

1 I have relied heavily for my observations on Homer's gods upon a few well-known studies by E. P. Dodds, Julian Jaynes, Joseph Russo, M. M. Willcock, and Bennett Simon.

ly squabbles. So when Zeus' first reaction to Thetis' request demonstrates a worried concern for what his wife will say (1.518) or when the crippled, gifted son intervenes to save the nagging mother from the bullying father (1.571), we understand. However much we would like to establish our own families on rational principles, we recognize that personal feelings, petty and otherwise, are usually the order of the day. Thus, Homer's system of anthropomorphic family members in heaven offers to man a very familiar, emotionally intelligible means of comprehending the irrational eternal powers which control the world.

Casting the almighty gods in the form of a large extended family does a great deal more than just emphasise the extent to which basic passions rule divine conduct and therefore are the motive forces in the world. Families, by their very nature, contain lines of authority, but the separation of powers and the ever-shifting allegiances within the family are never altogether clear. A family usually contains a dynamic life of its own, without an established logical formula which precisely defines the rights and duties of its members. We may recognize the father or the mother as the principal authority to whom we will ultimately, if necessary, defer, but in the meantime we assume, like all other members of the family, a right to get away with whatever we can in the frequently tense, fluid, emotionally ambiguous atmosphere of the clan. The assembly of the gods in the *Iliad* always remains a family with these familiar characteristics. The divine authority over the world becomes clear enough, but the spheres of influence in heaven and earth, the delineations of power, remain somewhat blurred, quite acceptably so, because the image of the family includes that sense of dynamically shifting uncertainty. The family metaphor, in other words, makes imaginatively acceptable the ambiguities and the irrationality of all-powerful rulers. No doubt that explains why the family is such an essential part of fiction, especially tragic drama. For example, King Lear's division of his kingdom into three parts, later two, is an incomprehensibly foolish political act of a powerful, experienced, and successful king, and if we saw only that in the opening scene of Shakespeare's play, then Lear might well forfeit a good deal of our sympathy; as a gesture from an authoritarian, egocentric, old man attempting to curry favour with his children in a self-dramatising family ritual, however, the action is perfectly understandable. In the same manner, the family metaphor works in the *Iliad* as the essential means of picturing the extent to which the entire cosmos operates by a constantly unpredictable, irrational, in some ways vaguely defined, but always imaginatively intelligible conflict.

The inherent ambiguity in the organizing metaphor of the divine family spares the reader the confusion he might experience if he were dealing with an apparently logical system which occasionally proved inconsistent (as in Milton's *Paradise Lost*, for example). In Homer's epic, since no rational principles govern the divine family, inconsistencies are not an imaginative problem. Poseidon can hate the Trojans and help the Akhaians; then he can turn around and save Aineias from Akhilleus (20.293). Emotional people behave this way all the time. Even when Zeus, whom we have more or less understood to be omnipotent, has to bow to the will of fate and abandon his grandson Sarpedon (16.433 ff.), or when Zeus holds up the scales to discover the outcome of Hektor's confrontation with Akhilleus (22.209), thus momentarily suggesting that the father of the gods is not omnipotent but serves the higher authority of fate, the cosmic order remains intact in our imaginations. For we have accepted the metaphysical system as a network of imprecise relationships among sharply etched divine personalities, whose individual authority does not require precise rational justification or clear definition. And the warriors in the epic do not abandon their faith in a capricious, often contradictory fate, because they know how large, passionate, powerful families conduct themselves. There it is quite common for the children to squabble viciously all the time while the temperamental patriarch looks on and laughs.

Moreover, the divine family in the *Iliad*, like a large human extended family, has no clearly defined limits to membership. The inner family circle governs the major action and receives most of the attention, but the extended family of the gods includes a host of personalities more or less closely related to the main group. Here again, we see little attempt to clarify specific relationships; the huge collection of divine, semi-divine, legendary, and human life exists as a vast interconnected nexus, with no consistently obvious and permanent lines of separation or connection. The main gods, of course, are eternal and possess extraordinary powers; between the gods and men, however, stretches a vague hierarchy of lesser deities--nymphs, semi-divine heroes, warriors with divine ancestors, and so forth. Some ramifications of the heavenly tree are clearly established, but the organism has countless tangled roots which extend themselves into all forms of life around man. These characteristics inherent in the metaphor indicate an essential similarity between Homer's metaphysical order and Greek religion, which is "not theologically fixed and stable, and [which] has no tradition of exclusion or finality: it is an open, not a closed system. There are no true gods and false, merely powers known and acknowledged since time immemorial, and new powers, newly experienced as active among men and newly acknowledged in worship. . . ." (Gould 8).

Hence, it can be quite misleading to talk, as I have earlier, of nature and the gods as if in the *Iliad* they are two distinct entities. Inheritors of a Christian culture in a scientific age, many of us have become accustomed to a vast gulf separating a mechanical nature from a living Creator. The relationship in Homer's poem, by contrast, stresses always that the divine personalities are fused with nature in a paradoxical but imaginatively vital manner. The gods both exist in nature and are nature; the Iliadic warriors maintain no clear distinction between the two states. The hawk that soars above the horizon may be a bird sent by a god, an omen indicating his intentions, or the transformed god himself, or both. The Skamander River is a river, a geographical feature, but it is also divine, not just the home or the favorite haunt of the god or a natural shrine to his worship, but the god himself, both natural object and divine personality. In the same way, the sea and Poseidon or Zeus and the sky are simultaneously two separate things and the same living presence. This point is most evident to us in the way in which the word Hades, even today, refers both to the Lord of the Underworld and to the underworld itself. For nature in the *Iliad* belongs in the family of gods, is infused with and an extension of the particular divine personalities, and is governed by the same passions as the heavenly rulers. The emotional intensity in the relationships between man and the gods thus rules man's interaction with nature as well.

In witnessing this feature of the *Iliad*, we can become aware of just how much vital imaginative contact with nature we have lost. But for all the intense beauty Homer's sense of the divine in nature might give to the world around man, we must be careful not to sentimentalize Homer's vision, not to view the poem through the rose-tinted glasses of nostalgic Romantic pantheism. For the gods in the *Iliad* may be instantly familiar as family members, and the divine vitality of nature may strike a welcome note to those long frustrated by thinking of nature as an alien resource, but the cosmic personalities have deadly powers and few compunctions about using them to gratify their intensely egoistic desires. Like the warriors fighting in the battles, we cannot forget that one constant preoccupation of this cosmic family is the destruction of men. We have already seen Apollo in action; the exchange between Hera and Zeus in the assembly in Book Four brings right to the forefront the passionate brutality of these gods. Early in the exchange Zeus declares to Hera:

> *"Could you breach the gates*
> *and the great walls yourself and feed on Priam*
> *with all his sons, and all the other Trojans,*
> *dished up raw, you might appease this rage!*
> *Do as you wish to do, then. This dispute*
> *should not leave rancor afterward between us.*
> *I must, however, tell you one thing more:*
> *remember it.*
>
> *Whenever my turn comes*

to lust for demolition of some city
whose people may be favorites of yours,
do not hamper my fury! Free my hands
as here I now free yours, my will prevailing
on my unwilling heart.

> *Of all the cites*

men of earth inhabit under the sun,
under the starry heavens, Ilion
stood first in my esteem, first in my heart,
as Priam did, the good lance, and his people.
My altar never lacked a feast at Troy
nor spilt wine, nor the smoke of sacrifice--
perquisites of the gods." (4.34)

Hera responds in kind:

> *"Dearest to me are these three cities:*
Mykênê of the broad lanes, Argos, Sparta.
Let them be pulled down, if you ever find them
hateful to you. I will not interfere.
I will not grudge you these." (4.51)

The scene introduces us unequivocally to the principles by which this all-powerful family operates. The acrimonious exchange between husband and wife displays towards man no particular benevolence. If this conversation represents the way in which the most important gods treat those dearest to them, the cities first in their esteem, civilized worshippers who have piously observed all the appropriate rites, we are surely entitled to wonder how any man is to secure their favour. We might note, in passing, how the family metaphor here enables man to accept the god's destructive actions and yet still retain a faith that Zeus has benevolent intentions sometimes. After all, he does manifest a certain reluctance. However, this first detailed glimpse of family life on Olympos shows how the petty bickering of these divine personalities has a very violent, selfish, and callous edge, with destruction for pious men a certain result. Remarkable also in the exchange is the normality of the scene; the reader gets the distinct impression that these fractious and destructive personalities conduct themselves in this way as a matter of course. The spite they display strikes us as a quotidian expression of the divine character. Significantly, Homer does not provide any specific motive in the conversation for Hera's attitude. The story provides him with a well-known reason, but Homer omits any reference to the Judgment of Paris, not, as one critic would have it, because it is "too abstract for his manner" (Griffin 25), but rather because it would give Hera a certain excuse and would thus detract from the most obviously shocking element in this death sentence for the Trojans, its casual and callous normality. The same inter-

43

preter has found this divine bargaining "unmotivated and mysterious" and has sought analogies in ancient Near Eastern rites (25). What gives the scene its impact, however, is surely not the mystery or lack of obviously irrational motivation, but the clarity of the picture. These gods do not move, as Jehovah does, in inscrutable ways; their personalities and passions are sharply defined. Their motives are their most immediate feelings, which they make no attempt to conceal.[2]

Obviously, faith in these deities requires a clear-eyed acceptance of irrational cosmic unpredictability and the frequently brutal consequences of that for man, without any sense of a divine agenda written up by some mysterious higher power on behalf of a chosen folk or in accordance with a moral covenant. One of the most remarkable features of the divine order in the *Iliad* is the way it demands from the men who believe in it--and all the warriors believe without question--the recognition of the universal power of irrational cosmic force. The warriors do not, like Job, demand an accounting from god, nor do they, like Job's friends, search for the sin they might have committed to earn the gods' displeasure. They rather accept unreasonable and inhumane afflictions as quite natural and continue to function, proud of their power to assert their own individuality. Whatever the possible historical origins of such a mythic system of faith, as we read the *Iliad* we can appreciate how a belief in the divine family as the formative metaphor defining natural and cosmic order prepares each warrior to accept as right whatever happens. With Zeus and his clan controlling the universe as a family activity, man can fully understand and emotionally accept the unpredictable shifts in an irrational fate.

The epic demonstrates, of course, that the gods' attitude to men is not consistently spiteful. The Olympians can provide decisive assistance and intimate practical counsel to individual men or transform the normal warrior into the great hero of the day. Zeus can grant Thetis' plea to avenge the insult to her son, and he can then with equally sudden indifference turn his back on the entire war and attend exclusively to his own affairs elsewhere (13.1). Or, in a different frame of mind, a god can express a sympathetic concern for the sufferings of humanity, unwelcome evils which the divine wills have brought about (see, for example, the speech of Zeus at 17.443). The capricious desires of the gods mean that

2 For G. S. Kirk there is nothing very shocking about the scene: "[Zeus' declaration of affection for Troy and Priam] may cause the listener to wonder why, nevertheless, he allows the city to fall, even after he has discharged his promise to Thetis. The answer is that this has been made inevitable by Paris' offense against hospitality, which is protected by Zeus ... himself, and by the Trojans' condoning of it by receiving him and Helen (<u>Commentary</u> 333). Chapter 7 discusses the possible origins and effects of such a cut-and-dried view of Homer's poem.

the only consistent feature of their relationship with man is their unpredictability. From a caring protector of a pampered favorite, any god can instantly change his role, for no particular reason, suddenly withdrawing his support to become a cruel deceiver of the same man's hopes and an agent in his brutal destruction. In their constant interference with man, the gods display nothing we can recognize as a divine concern for a reasonable principle of justice (Dodds 32). In fact, if we want to use the word "justice" to describe what goes on in the *Iliad*, we must divest it of its customary meanings for us, so that when we speak of divine justice we mean some tautological principle that decisive things happen because they happen. Homer reminds us of this fundamental condition of life with the frequent and poetically effective divine epithets. Those which describe Zeus, for example, ("son of crooked-minded Krónos," "inscrutable," "whose joy is lightning," "who bears the stormcloud for a shield," and so forth) keep reverberating through the images of human effort and hope the ominous sense of an irrational, almighty cosmic destiny.

Occasionally the *Iliad* will mention the notion of a moralized fate, that is, a sense that the cosmic justice of Zeus does operate by some ethical principle, in the way that the *Odyssey* repeatedly brings out. One should note, however, that such suggestions typically come from one of the warriors, not so much as a statement of belief as a wish that heavenly justice were not so irrational. When Menelaos prays to Zeus for victory over Paris on the ground that Paris has broken a law of hospitality (3.351), the injured husband is not invoking holy law but expressing a personal wish. Hence, when Zeus denies his prayer, as he does so often in the poem, Menelaos does not question his faith but reaffirms it. He had no right to expect that his plea for moral reasonableness would move Zeus. Similarly, immediately before Akhilleus returns to avenge Patroklos, he momentarily wishes that the fatal condition of life might change to something less irrational and destructive. He expresses his deepest desires in some of the most eloquent lines in the entire epic.

> "*Ai! let strife and rancor*
> *perish from the lives of gods and men,*
> *with anger that envenoms even the wise*
> *and is far sweeter than slow-dripping honey,*
> *clouding the hearts of men like smoke....*" *(18.107)*

Of these lines Herakleitos noted: "Homer was wrong.... He did not see that he was praying for the destruction of the universe; for, if his prayer were heard, all things would pass away" (qtd Burnet 136). But Homer does not utter this prayer; Akhilleus does. His vain demand for a life more peaceful and reasonable, like the earlier prayer of Menelaos, emphasises that the hopes of men, even the most powerful, cannot alter the basic conditions of Zeus' rule that there are no reasonable moral rules. And to wish that condition away, as Herakleitos notes and as Akhilleus also realizes, is to wish away the nature of the world.[3]

III

The shaping control the gods exercise over the conduct of the war takes place in a number of ways. The most remarkable is the constant and direct divine interference in the common events of the battlefield. The precise behaviour of the gods may be impossible to predict, but for the warriors the actions of the heavenly powers affect almost everything that happens. The gods, in other words, have not just established warfare as the condition of man's life; they also determine the decisive events in the day-to-day actions of the combat. The fatalistic sense which enables the warriors to come to terms with their perilous life, their faith in the cosmic family, also accounts for the significant incidents in a particular fray. The fortunes of war thus depend not so much on luck, human resourcefulness, or obedience to holy commandments as on the capricious desires of external divine agents. Just as events in the natural world continuously reveal the presence of divinities, so the success or failure in the front lines indicates the working of the higher powers.

The divine influence on human actions typically takes one of two forms, a direct interference in a physical or a mental event. In the former, the god acts to guide a spear or an arrow to the right target or away from the intended victim, to cause some equipment, like a chin strap or an axle, to break, to trip a runner, and in general to make sure that the incidents of the melee fit his desires for that particular moment. Whatever happens around the warrior on the battlefield, therefore, especially any-

---

3 The strongest suggestion of a divine moral scheme occurs in Book Sixteen, in a passage which refers to Zeus' anger at those who "enforce their crooked judgments and banish justice from the market place, thoughtless of gods' vengeance" (16.386). The passage offers such a marked contrast to the whole tenor of the Iliad that it has inevitably invited the notion that it is a later interpolation. See, for example, the detailed comments by Paley (2:140). If we wish to avoid the debate about interpolation, we can properly appeal to the critical principle of inclusiveness: "If understanding is a matter of fitting parts into a whole, then that belief about their relations will be superior which can encompass the most elements in the configuration it projects" (Armstrong 346).

thing unexpected, does not happen by accident but by divine desire. In Book Three, for example, Menelaos finally gets his wish to face Paris; Menelaos feels he deserves to defeat Paris and has the physical superiority over his adversary. But his sword shatters--to Menelaos clearly the work of Zeus ("O Father Zeus, of all the gods, none is more cruel to hopeful men than you are!" 3.365)--and then, a moment later, when Menelaos is about to break Paris' neck, Aphrodite makes sure that Paris escapes back to Troy in safety. In the normal course of events, Menelaos should have dispatched Paris quickly; the unexpected outcome must clearly result from divine interference.[4]

More complex than the physical interference of the gods are those moments when they suddenly and decisively, for better or worse, interact with human minds and emotions. The warriors in the *Iliad* do not share our traditional faith in the importance of the unique inner character, which shapes so much of the way we think about ourselves and fellow human beings, because for them all extraordinary human attributes and actions come, not from individual character, but from divine agents external to man. The gods routinely alter a warrior's normal behaviour and his human perceptual processes. Dreams come from Zeus, as we see in the opening of Book Two. And the gods can send an idea into a man's head (8.218). Alternatively, they can assume the shape of a familiar mortal and deliver an unusual message or perform an important task. In the course of the poem Apollo does this repeatedly: as Akamas (5.460), as Mentes (17.71), as Periphas (17.322), as Lykaon (20.79), and as Agenor (21.600). Thus, the unpredictable irrationality of heaven freely enters into human behaviour at every turn, and there is no permanently clear demarcation between normal human conduct and divinely affected human conduct. When Homer informs us that a particular god has entered or interfered with a warrior, for example, the expression means both that the warrior has become temporarily changed in some way (for example, braver or more aggressive than usual) and that some external agent, a god, has effected the process.

Given that this view of human action apparently differs considerably from our own, we might begin to explore the consequences of it for an understanding of the conduct of the warriors. At the simplest level, the fatalistic view of divine interference fosters the belief that people do not

---

4 We recognize a similar belief when a modern soldier affirms the fatalistic sense that somewhere or other there is a shell or bullet with his name on it, or when, faced with the chaos of the killing zone, we declare that there are no atheists in foxholes. Giving a name and a motive to the unpredictable destructive forces which threaten him is one of the soldier's most important means of emotionally comprehending what might otherwise be an insupportably meaningless endeavour.

bear the responsibility for what they are. Telamonian Aias is a redoubtable soldier because he has received "a powerful great frame . . . as a gift from god, and a clear head" (7.288), and Akhilleus' skills come from "the gods who live forever" (1.290). Helen recognizes that she and Paris have no control over or responsibility for what they are, their "portion, all of misery, given by Zeus" (6.357). Paris has no choice in the matter of his character. The gods have made him the way he is, and he and the others must accept the fact.

> *"My own gifts are from pale-gold Aphrodítê--*
> *do not taunt me for them. Glorious things*
> *the gods bestow are not to be despised,*
> *being as the gods will: wishing will not bring them."* *(3.64)*

Beyond that, by a natural extension of the same notion, the individuals do not bear the responsibility for the unusual actions they carry out, because anything out of the ordinary must come from a divine agent. The next chapter examines the heroic code, the community ethic by which these soldiers establish rules for normal behaviour, but we need to appreciate first that in the *Iliad* actions that transgress the norm must have an external cause. When Akhilleus, quite unexpectedly, does not physically defend his honour before the insults of Agamemnon, the obvious reason is that some god has prevented him from doing so. In such a situation, the warrior must obey the god: "when you two immortals speak, a man complies, though his heart burst" (1.216). The normal behaviour in the group would demand from Akhilleus a different response; since his reaction here is extraordinary, a god must have been at work. Similarly, Agamemnon's enormous mistake in treating Akhilleus badly must have an external cause. Although Agamemnon's conduct deprives the Akhaians of the services of Akhilleus and the Myrmidons and thus has dire results for the army and although the king must eventually offer suitable reparations, he bears no personal inner responsibility for his actions.

> *"The Akhaians often brought this up against me,*
> *and chided me. But I am not to blame.*
> *Zeus and Fate and a nightmare Fury are,*
> *for putting savage Folly in my mind*
> *in the assembly that day, when I wrested*
> *Akhilleus' prize of war from him. In truth,*
> *what could I do? Divine will shapes these things.*
> *Ruinous Folly, eldest daughter of Zeus,*
> *beguiles us all. Her feet are soft, from walking*
> *not on earth but over the heads of men*
> *to do them hurt."* *(19.85)*

No one challenges this assessment. Agamemnon receives some stinging criticism in the course of the battles (for example, at 14.83) but not on this occasion. For here he speaks what everyone acknowledges to be true. Similarly, when, by firing an arrow at Menelaos, Pandaros destroys all hope that the war might be resolved, he does so under the divine compulsion of Athena's "leading him on, the foolish man, to folly" (4.104). Even Helen, the famous legendary cause of the war, had no personal hand in the events which initiate doom for the Trojans. King Priam, who ought to know better than anyone else exactly what the war is costing his people, directs no anger at Helen.

> *"You are not to blame,*
> *I hold the gods to blame for bringing on*
> *this war against the Akhaians, to our sorrow."* (3.164)

Extraordinary conduct on the battlefield also has a divine origin. The gods can interfere in such a way as to invest a warrior with unusually heroic powers, temporarily transforming a typical leader into an invincible conqueror. Once again, the action of the god occurs for no clear reason, beyond the god's immediate desire to assist a favorite. In this, as in so much else in the poem, the conduct of Diomedes is typical.

> *Now Diomêdês' hour for great action came.*
> *Athêna made him bold, and gave him ease*
> *to tower amid Argives, to win glory,*
> *and on his shield and helm she kindled fire*
> *most like midsummer's purest flaming star*
> *in heaven rising, bathed by the Ocean stream.*
> *So fiery she made his head and shoulders*
> *as she impelled him to the center where*
> *the greatest number fought.* (5.1)

In the fighting which follows, Diomedes enjoys an unusual series of personal victories. Athena helps him instantly to recover from an arrow wound and fires his spirits for even more combat, in which he acts for a while as an invincible killing machine. His opponents recognize that some god must be at work in this unusually successful ferocity: "If it be Diomêdês, never could he have made this crazy charge without some god behind him" (5.184). The inspired hero pushes his divinely assisted force at the enemy, even challenging and wounding Aphrodite, who significantly is reminded by Zeus that she, as goddess of erotic love, does not belong on the field, until Diomedes' present course reaches a limit once he has, with Athena's assistance, confronted Ares. At that point he rejoins the Argive forces as the normal warrior leader he was before. This example illustrates a recurring phenomenon in the poem, the *aristeia*, when the warrior, with the help of a god, is transformed from a leader among equals to a temporarily pre-eminent battlefield victor. In the *aristeia* the warrior's usual behaviour changes; he becomes abnormally ferocious, beautiful, and successful. Therefore, some divine presence has clearly worked upon him. In exactly the same way, the gods can fill a character with erotic passion and metamorphose him or her into a supremely desireable love partner. Helen has no power finally to resist the demands of Aphrodite, any more than Paris can resist the erotic impulse to make love to Helen. Questions about whether or not they ought to surrender to love while the Trojans perish in defense of the city simply do not make sense.

Iliadic man has, in other words, a fatalistic sense of his own inner life, and the ironic forces which govern heaven, nature, and the war thus play a decisive role in his understanding of himself. As many critics have observed, we are dealing with characters who do not think of themselves in the same way we normally do. They lack an inner moral consciousness which enables them to reflect, evaluate, and decide what to do. Instead they respond directly to the immediate situation in which they find themselves or, in unusual behaviour, to the dictates of divine agents external to themselves. This lack of self-conscious inner individuality, of that quality which usually forms the basis for our judgments about people, may be the main reason why the characters in the *Iliad* all seem in some essential way the same. Some are bigger, run faster, or throw further than others; some are grizzled, others have red hair, and so on, but they differ little from each other in any significant inner quality, and thus we cannot easily make the usual discriminations we do with people. Just as it is impossible simply to judge Homer's war as good or bad, so one cannot apply common moral judgments to the warriors, whose behaviour arises out of the same fated, external, ironic conflict of cosmic agents as does the war.

Of course, we do get some sense of differences in the characters; most readers, for example, have strong reservations about Agamemnon's conduct in one or two places and like Hektor and Menelaos (who seems occasionally a favorite of the narrator's). But, for the most part, the characters differ little from each other in their mental or physical identities. If one were casting a film of the *Iliad*, what significant criteria could one use, apart from the very occasional hints about personal appearance, to distinguish between, say, Antenor, Sarpedon, Diomedes, Meriones, Helenos, Glaukos, Hektor, Menelaos, Agamemnon, or Odysseus? Fine discriminations between them would be impossible because our evaluation of the warriors does not arise from any intimate feeling for their inner moral qualities, which they do not possess, or from any significant differences in their individual sensibilities, but rather from our response to their actions, which are all very similar, the only major difference being one of degree. As Erich Auerbach points out in his famous essay on Homer, the characters are all basically the same (10). For Homer's main emphasis always falls, not on the significant qualitative differences between men, but upon the fatal situation common to them all.

> *"Friends," one would say,*
> *"whether you are among the best, or fair,*
> *or a poor fighter--all men cannot be*
> *equal in war--this challenge is for everyone;*
> *you see it for yourselves." (12.269)*

Perhaps for this reason the remarks of some commentators who try to read the *Iliad* as if it were a conventional popular novel, who seek, that is, to trace in the events the subtle shifts of inner feelings and thoughts of delicately drawn, unique characters, can occasionally sound unnecessarily fussy and misplaced.[5]

If the Homeric warriors' habit of seeing in external forces the source of significant human actions and of denying any rich complexity of inner life differs fundamentally from modern conceptions of human behaviour, then how do we understand them? How, that is, do we account for the significance of their actions? If, as I suggested in Chapter 1, interpretation is an unmediated conversation between the present sensibility of the reader and the strangeness of the ancient text, then how can we imaginatively accept Homeric characterization without recourse to a study of the history of psychology or religion? On the other hand, if the poem is to speak to us fully, we must be careful not to evade or to neutralize the immediate impact of this vision of human life by assigning it to an early stage in the history of man's mental development, or by placing the phenomenon in a box marked primitive myth, or by simply dismissing it as mental instability or schizophrenia, all of which views, however interesting and historically important, can tend to persuade the reader that the behaviour of the Iliadic warriors has no immediate relevance to modern concerns. Our desire to distance ourselves from Homeric psychology may, after all, stem in large part from an inability or an unwillingness to recognize our own faces in Homer's mirror.

We might begin by acknowledging that we have all experienced a sense of acting without reflection, of carrying out something remarkably good or foolish under an impulse, particularly when under stress, so

---

5 For example, the following comment by Malcolm Willcock on 6.518: "Paris thinks only of himself and tries by this unnecessary self-criticism to improve his brother's opinion of him. Hektor in reply speaks more kindly, realizing that Paris has been hurt by his criticisms in 326 ff. This is all very human" (Companion).

that when we look back on what we have done, we talk of being inspired, deluded, or compelled to complete an action, especially one that falls outside our normal behaviour. And we are usually at a loss to explain how we could have done such an act. The literature of warfare, in particular, presents countless examples of extraordinary conduct in the front-lines, heroism, cowardice, and atrocity, for which the agents have no reasonable explanations. Few things are more painful for us than to put one of own soldiers on trial for acts committed in the killing zone. In such cases, we demand a rational moral evaluation of conduct obviously originating from passionate sources beyond the reach of our most fundamental metaphors of how the mind operates. We are so wedded to the notion of self-consciousness that we need to assign personal responsibility; in spite of the evidence, we do not like to credit the sometimes extraordinary efficacy of powerful, spontaneous, and impersonal forces beyond our control.

Our traditional theories of the mind may inform us that irrational motive forces come from within according to some as yet unknown interaction between the mind and the body, but our language often suggests otherwise. We still talk of artists being inspired by the Muse, of athletes have God in their corner, of gamblers escorting Lady Luck, of worshippers being filled with the Holy Spirit, of travellers going where the spirit moves them. Some twenty years ago, the comedian Flip Wilson made a fortune on television with his slogan "The Devil made me do it." We laughed at the excuse, but we knew exactly what he meant. Indeed, the similarity between the behaviour of the Homeric warriors and athletes competing in stressful team competition often prompts natural comparisons of Iliadic warfare and modern professional sports (for example, M. S. Silk 103). When we discuss and evaluate athletic team competitions, we tend to concentrate much less on the moral qualities or uniquely personal characteristics of the individual participants than on their external actions and the effects of the situation upon those actions, often stressing the importance of the unpredictable and imponderable factors outside the control of the individuals.

The Homeric vision of human motivation becomes clearer perhaps when we consider the behaviour of young children. A child tends to respond instantly to an impulse, from whatever quarter, and often finds himself quite unable to explain why he has acted in a certain way. He has no consciousness of a motive, for his action was an immediate response to an irresistible urge for which he feels no personal responsibility, since it was not part of him. Parents spend many, many years teaching the child the notion of the self, the idea that he has an inner consciousness which directs his actions and which makes him personally accountable for what he does. The lesson usually takes hold very slowly, for the natural resistance to the modern psychological metaphors exerts a strong opposition. If the child does not learn the lesson, however, he can have great trouble functioning in a modern society which bases its social relationships on well-controlled lies and on delayed emotional responses, its educational, legal, and moral systems on the notions of personal responsibility, guilt, and individual self-consciousness, and its business and political ethics on the survival values of deceit.

The analogy between the impulsive, non-conscious behaviour of the Homeric warrior and the actions of modern children may explain why so many readers find something childlike and immature in the actions of the Iliadic characters. The warriors are so immediately impulsive and candid about their feelings, without the guile we often associate with maturity. No human being in the *Iliad* tells a successful lie. That would require a consciousness, an inner awareness of the difference between the spoken facts and the truth. No one has any inner secrets. The closest we come to any form of double-dealing is Odysseus' treatment of Dolon in Book Ten or Hektor's momentary thought of breaking the code in Book Twenty-two. In the *Iliad* characters do not engage in deception, not even in those tricks common to modern warfare. They cannot even carry out the first lesson we have to teach our impulsive young, the delayed emotional response; hence, Akhilleus's extraordinary restraint in Book One must be god inspired. There is no room in the *Iliad* for the celebrated sly resourcefulness of Odysseus in the *Odyssey*, because what people in the *Iliad* say and what they do are spontaneous responses to the way they feel in a particular situation. Those who see Odysseus in the *Iliad* as having much of the same comic resourcefulness he displays in the later epic (for example, Whitman 176) surely overlook the fact that Odysseus acts throughout as a loyal and inflexible apologist for the warrior ethic, energetically and openly correcting the doubts of Thersites in 2.246 and of Agamemnon in 14.82 and of himself in 11.404. Homer uses Odysseus, famous in legend from the days of Homer's audience to the present as a tricky, ingeniously inventive, often deceitful adventurer, to emphasise through the ironic contradictions between his reputation and his behaviour in the *Iliad* the absence of such non-heroic qualities in Iliadic society.[6]

6   The brief portrayal of Akhilleus in the Odyssey, in the scene where the great hero of the war epic criticizes the warrior ethic, serves the same function of bringing out the qualities of a particular view of life by contradicting our traditional associations with a famous hero.

To describe the warriors' actions and their understanding of themselves as immature or childish, however, summons up an unnecessarily pejorative judgment. The conduct may appear to us very odd in some ways, not because we have outgrown it, but rather because we customarily deny our innate ability to understand our actions as spontaneously prompted by external force; we have a different conceptual metaphor.[7] The point I wish to stress is that it takes no great leap of imagination to sense within ourselves a response to life similar to the Homeric vision, and there is certainly plenty of reliable evidence that when we have to deal with a significant emotional experience, like war, love, or sports, many of us quickly revert to a faith in cosmic forces at work all around us. Reading the *Iliad* can thus imaginatively remind us of an understanding of human nature quite foreign to our orthodox ways of analyzing our conduct but very familiar to our feelings about ourselves and the world. If in that process, the poem stimulates us to re-examine the adequacy of our modern concept of self-consciousness, so much the better for us.

In any event, the images of divine intervention in significant matters of human behaviour bring out how Iliadic man must constantly respond to the forces of ambiguous and irrational gods. The warrior's personality is thus part of a natural world ruled by conflict. The men glory, suffer, and die in a fatalistic world from which conventional notions of justice and moral judgments have been excluded because they are literally inconceivable. Without divine reasonableness or a covenant, justice is merely the given irrationality of things; without self-consciousness, there can be no sin, only actions more or less under the influence of external agents. None of this means that man is a mere automaton, a limp feather to be blown around by contending divine whims. For he has the freedom and the will to assert himself in the face of his paradoxical destiny, in the full awareness that the only certainty in a cosmos full of divinely inspired strife is his own death.

> With Homer there is no marvelling or blaming, and no answer is expected. Who is good in the Iliad? Who is bad? Such distinctions do not exist; there are only men suffering, warriors fighting, some winning, some losing. The passion for justice emerges only in a mourning for justice, in the dumb avowal of silence. To condemn force, or absolve it, would be to condemn, or absolve, life itself. (Bespaloff 48)

---

7 The philosophical and psychological adequacy of our orthodox ways of understanding the mind has, in recent years, been seriously challenged by many writers, notably by Gilbert Ryle, Richard Rorty, and José Delgado, among many others.

CHAPTER 4

The Heroic Code

"Man imitates in action his vision of the nature of things." (George Grant)

I

Consider the following analogy. Let us imagine that civilization consists of a large group of different families on board a ship in a stormy sea. The situation presents daily perils from the natural forces that threaten at every moment to overturn the craft and drown everyone. What should the people do? We might, from our vantage, suggest a number of options available to them, but the response that will make the best sense to them, the one they will inevitably use to organize their control of the vessel, will depend upon how they interpret the forces which threaten their existence. If, for example, those on board believe that there is some means of predicting, manipulating, and using--even inexpertly and intermittently--the natural forces to their advantage in order to survive the ravages of the tempest and to reach a safe haven, then they will act to maximize their survival chances by applying all the individual and collective human resourcefulness they can muster--adjusting the sails, tacking, changing the ballast, devising special sails, sheltering in a lee water, and so on. Many may die, but they will be the unfortunate sacrifices the society has to make to outlast the storm. Alternatively, if the sailors believe that there is no safe haven but that the tempest operates by some discernable pattern which takes into account the daily conduct of the members of the community, then they will pay considerable attention to the rules of behaviour which, in part, govern the external threats to their well being, obviously seeking to avoid those errors which, they think, will cause the ocean to pluck them from the deck or swallow the ship up entirely. Or, again, if the seafarers believe that the storm acts as a distraction from a more important reality which they can discover only by prolonged study in preparation for a finer existence after drowning, they will probably spend less time trimming the sails and more time concentrating on their solitary exercises or group prayer below decks. Clearly, before the group on board can do anything effective, its members need to discover and to act upon a common way of comprehending their situation, for if they can reach no consensus about the storm, then the group will cease to function as a community and will fall apart into disputatious sects which may well kill each other before the sea does.

In each of the above cases, and one can think of a number of others, the basic metaphor is fatalistic, for the deadly storm, the sea, and the ship remain given, but the human responses to the situation vary with the fundamental assumptions about the nature of reality. And any particular response appears foolish or evil to someone who does not imaginatively share the assumptions upon which it rests. To grasp why particular people respond in a particular way, then, we need to examine their vision of the nature of things, for we comprehend the significance of their behaviour only when we see the beliefs which naturally prompt it. For example, if we wish to apply the above analogy to the *Iliad*, we might characterize the warriors as men who see no end to the perilous storm, no reasonable pattern in the tempest or in the deaths it occasions, no present or future haven, and no life after drowning in the sea. They use the familiar metaphor of the divine, extended, anthropomorphic family to provide themselves a means of comprehending what is going on and why, so that they can articulate a response to their condition, but this shaping pattern of belief, by its irrational character, does not enable them to justify their efforts to cope with the daily mortal dangers they face. Since any notion of cosmic justice or rational purpose is wholly absent from the natural and heavenly order, the warriors must discover in themselves, in their response to the situation, a sense of purpose and a system of values, without which their community will disintegrate into a nihilistic, absurd existence.

Simple analogies can, of course, mislead as easily as they can illuminate, but the one above introduces an essential point we must understand about the Iliadic warriors: their sense that they have nowhere else to go. They do not want to fight, but they have no choice. No safe haven awaits, and they have neither lifeboats nor a convenient exit from the ship. For all the glory it brings, these soldiers do not like the war particularly. If the world offered an alternative, they would prefer to take it. But since they have no option, they accept the condition with a grim candour.

> *"We must do service, too. That is the way*
> *the Lord Zeus burdened us when we were born." (10.70)*

> *"O Father Zeus, incomparable*
> *they say you are among all gods and men*
> *for wisdom; yet this battle comes from you."* *(13.631)*

> *"Our lot from youth to age*
> *was given us by Zeus: danger and war*
> *to wind upon the spindle of our years*
> *until we die to the last man."* *(14.85)*

Even the best-known evocation of the warrior's fighting creed, the speech of Sarpedon to Glaukos, makes the point that the glories of the warrior life would not be worth it, if human beings had a better alternative.

> *"Ah, cousin, could we but survive this war*
> *to live forever deathless, without age,*
> *I would not ever go again to battle,*
> *nor would I send you there for honor's sake!*
> *But now a thousand shapes of death surround us,*
> *and no man can escape them, or be safe."* *(12.322)*

If life were not life, Sarpedon asserts, he would not fight. Whatever pride he takes in his standing as a mighty leader, Sarpedon can imagine how much finer human existence would be if the universal conditions were different. Even those who do find a temporary escape from the terror of war by offering ransom, like the two sons of Priam, Isos and Antiphos, are later killed (11.101). Human beings cannot escape the war. The eagerness with which the soldiers stream to the ships in Book Two, under the mistaken impression that they are going home, indicates that, whatever is keeping the armies before Troy, it is not an unalloyed pleasure in the fighting. Both sides share an equally intense desire for peace.

> *Meanwhile the soldiers held their hands to heaven,*
> *Trojans and Akhaians, in this prayer:*

> *"Father Zeus, almighty over Ida,*
> *may he who brought this trouble on both sides*
> *perish! Let him waste away*
> *into the undergloom! As for ourselves,*
> *let us be loyal friends in peace!"* *(3.318)*

In their hearts the men might desire a cessation of combat ("Now all hearts lifted at his words, for both sides hoped for an end of miserable war" 3.111), but any attempt to bring the war to a halt, like the truce in Book Four, will fail, because such an event contradicts the given conditions of the world.

57

almighty and most glorious! Gods undying!
Let any parties to this oath who first
calamitously break it have their brains
decanted like these wine-drops on the ground--
they and their children; let their wives be slaves."

The oath ran so, but Zeus would not abide
by what they swore. (3.298)

To comprehend the warrior code, then, we must see it as a response to what the men perceive as the inescapable, perilous, fated condition of human life. The only certainties are constant war and inevitable death. Turning one's back on the endeavour or trying to walk away from the fighting group simply guarantees that death will come sooner rather than later. Those who run from the fight get speared in the back.

The warrior's sense of his fatal condition expresses itself in his religious attitudes. He diligently worships the gods who will, he knows, keep the war going forever and destroy all men in turn, no matter how they behave. Such piety requires an extraordinarily tough acceptance of an unreasonable fate, and all the characters in the *Iliad* have the courage and energy to believe in and to celebrate their faith in a harsh universe. They approach their gods with a clear idea of what life has in store for them. The prayers and formulaic oaths express an acute sense of the individual's chances in this mortal coil, and the subjunctive mood declares the extent of the warrior's confidence in favorable treatment: "Honor the gods' will, they may honor ours" (1.218). For these worshippers accept the fact that the gods will probably disappoint their most cherished hopes, but they do not therefore cease to believe. A prayer for divine assistance may be answered. Perhaps the gods may even relent and brings things to an end with a final victory or a permanent truce.

"What is to come? Bad days again
in the bloody lines? Or can both sides be friends?
Which will it be from Zeus, who holds the keys
and rationing of war?" (4.82)

This stance is not like Pascal's wager that, since we do not know whether there is life after death or not, we had better play it safe, for the warriors know they have nothing to win from the gods in a later life. Their attitude rather expresses a hard, open-eyed acceptance of the given condition of life on its own terms. In their religious practices, the warriors endorse and celebrate the fatal ironies of their existence. Hence, military disaster, the clearest evidence that the rulers of heaven and earth are not heedful of the warriors' prayers, does not shake their faith in the gods who have on this occasion ignored and disappointed them. When the Trojans triumph over the Akhaians, Agamemnon does not question his earlier sacrifices; he accepts the fact that on this day "Zeus's mood has changed; he cares for Hektor's offerings more than ours" (10.45). Perhaps tomorrow fortunes will reverse themselves and perhaps not. For who knows how the gods, who determine the war, will act?

With this awareness of his common lot, the Homeric warrior elects to live as fully as he can, to stand up in the battle line, celebrating his individual ability to confront his inevitable destiny fearlessly for as long as he lasts. Since there is no escape from the war and death, he will impose on the battle his own presence, declaring by his brave stance before the enemy and the irrational powers of fate that he counts for something. Unlike many celebrated fighters of later ages, the Homeric leader does not put his life on the line for a political or religious cause. He does not fight in defense of his homeland or of his freedom from barbarian rule. Even the oath to Agamemnon or the security of Troy matters less than the individual's sense of his own personal stature, which he can only protect and enhance by standing in the front lines fighting openly alongside the best men and against the worthiest opponents.

> *"No invitation*
> *to dance, that shouting, but to a fight.*
>
> > *No plan,*
> *no cleverness can serve us now but this:*
> *to close with them and fight with all we have.*
> *Better to win life or to lose it fighting*
> *now, once and for all, than to be bled*
> *to death by slow degrees in grinding war*
> *against these ships, by lesser men than we." (15.508)*

Those who survive to reach old age are, paradoxically, unlucky, for they cannot share the fighting stature of the younger warriors. They win no glory because, as Priam states, they have no strength to resist and thus become merely helpless victims of the war. No old man wins fresh glory in death.

> > *"Everything done*
> *to a young man killed in war becomes his glory,*
> *once he is riven by the whetted bronze:*
> *dead though he be, it is all fair, whatever*
> *happens then. But when an old man falls,*
> *and dogs disfigure his grey head and cheek*
> *and genitals, that is most harrowing*
> *of all that men in their hard lives endure." (22.71)*

Thus, the Iliadic man fights because in a contingent, hostile universe he wants his life to mean something. If he cannot establish his worth as an individual, the only alternative is to accept the passive anonymity of the non-combatant. In that sense, the men do have a choice, as Akhilleus does. But if they want to stamp their life with any notion of worth, then they must go to war. The men who paid money to avoid the war are denied the chance to prove their value as human beings. The Akhaian Eukhenor has to come to the war or to face a long deadly sickness at home. He comes to the war, is killed by Paris, and thus avoids "the heavy fine men paid who stayed at home, and the long pain of biding mortal illness" (13.669). The fine and the illness here are not just a financial loss and a physical ailment but the spiritual sickness of anonymity in a world where one's value emerges only in battle. The warrior does not want to die; he would prefer an existence where he could escape that unwelcome event, especially since death is the end of everything. But, like all men, he wants his life to have some purpose, not miserable insignificance but an enduring value, and if he must die violently in order to achieve that, then he will live as gloriously as he can, even if the effort brings on death much more quickly than inaction, for only through his personal valour as a soldier will his life mean anything.

> Even though life is transient--in part because it is so--one may give it the permanence of renown. And the static quality of the chief characters is a way of showing that if a man is to achieve this immortality he must choose one course of action rather than another. Through his choice, of course, he gives up the infinite possibility on which the characters of Hamlet or Prufrock are based; he renounces it in order to wrest something from the finite and actual which will not be merely fleeting. The result for the Iliad is, if we consider this one quality apart from the rest of the poem, a simple concept of character. But far more significantly the result is a "placing" of man, a showing of the way in which his glory and his limitations combine. (Knight 37)

The society in the *Iliad*, therefore, commits itself to the search for individual achievement in battle. What a warrior can win in combat defines his worth to the group and, beyond that, to the irrational universe. By demonstrating his superiority over other men in the supreme test of hand-to-hand fighting, the Homeric warrior gives his individual existence a purpose and confirms in his own eyes that his life has significance, for only in that way can he acquire what openly shows his value as a human being, his public status, a preoccupation with which governs his every action. His value to his peers and therefore his sense of himself are based upon his ability to fight, and his worth as a fighter depends not only upon his god-given physical attributes but also upon the number of soldiers he leads, his past record, his family's reputation, and the quantity and quality of his weapons--the public attributes which announce the esteem in which his comrades and his enemies hold him.

The social group organizes and controls the behaviour of its members through the conventions of status. In the stressful melee, appeals to each man's status unite the soldiers and bolster their courage.

> *"Be men, dear friends, respect yourselves as men*
> *before the others! All of you, remember*
> *children and wives, possessions, and your parents,*
> *whether they be alive or dead! I beg you,*
> *on their account, although they are not here,*
> *to hold your ground: no panic and no rout!"* *(15.661)*

Nestor here makes no promises of safety, no appeals to the justice of their cause or their group promise to Agamemnon, no reminders of how nasty the Trojans can be, no reference to a glorious afterlife in Hades or to the importance of defending home and hearth--none of the traditional appeals from generals to their troops. He reminds the men of what they are, urging them to live up to the value they have acquired, their standing in the eyes of the world, their status. For Nestor, the most experienced warrior in the Argive forces, understands that in an undertaking as metaphysically irrational and as emotionally and physically stressful as the war before Troy, the warrior's principal motivation comes from a desire to maintain his value in the eyes of the group; without that, he could not face the terror.

Obviously, such an emphasis on status can only work if there exists an appropriate relationship between the individual and the other members of the society. The Iliadic warriors share a common value system and therefore agree on what constitutes merit. They can, in the normal course of events, quickly resolve arguments by an appeal to the customary unwritten rules. In seeking to arbitrate the initial quarrel, for example, Nestor admits that the gods have given Akhilleus a military prowess greater than Agamemnon's; however, he urges Akhilleus to follow the king's orders because Agamemnon leads more troops and therefore has a higher status. Agamemnon's authority from Zeus rests on his "power over men" (1.281). Nireos may be the most beautifully made leader after Akhilleus, but he is "a feeble man" because he leads "a small contingent" (2.675). The demands of the group also require that a warrior never stray too far from his peers, for the society must always retain a sense of its identity and remind each warrior of his particular place in it. Hence, the constant appeal of mass display. Only by an overt public group show can the society affirm the importance of what it is doing and overcome any potential disillusionment with the endeavour. The famous parade of the contingents in Book Two, for example, which originates in a suggestion from Nestor about how to deal with the crisis in morale among the Argive troops, serves not only to list the participants, but also to demonstrate in public the group's solidarity at a critical moment. The frequent religious rituals, prayers, and assemblies have the same purpose: they assert the communal identity and provide an occasion when each warrior can confirm and celebrate his worth, publicly recognize the status of each of his allies, and, in turn, be recognized by them. Any doubts about the war disappear in the mass display.

This feature of the *Iliad* stands in marked contrast to the *Odyssey*, in which a great many group activities, particularly feasting and entertainment, celebrate the joys of social interaction for its own sake and where the identity of each person is less important than the conventions of civilized hospitality. The name and the status of a guest, for example, can emerge during the leisurely social event rather than being fiercely declared right at the outset of an encounter. In the *Odyssey*, Odysseus, who has a very strong sense of his status, will conceal it or lie about it as an appropriate stratagem. In the *Iliad*, by contrast, candid public assertions of status are the constant preoccupation of the warrior's life, so that when he moves from the assembly and the parade, when the time for action arrives, his confident sense of his social importance in and out of war spurs him to face the danger bravely, as Sarpedon observes in our earliest and most famous statement of the warrior's faith.

> *"What is the point of being honored so*
> *with precedence at table, choice of meat,*
> *and brimming cups, at home in Lykia,*
> *like gods at ease in everyone's regard?*
> *And why have lands been granted you and me*
> *on Xánthos' bank: to each his own demesne,*
> *with vines and fields of grain?*
>
>   *So that we two*
> *at times like this in the Lykian front line*
> *may face the blaze of battle and fight well,*
> *that Lykian men-at-arms may say:*
> *'They are no common men, our lords who rule*
> *in Lykia. They eat fat lamb at feasts*
> *and drink rare vintages, but the main thing is*
> *their fighting power, when they lead in combat!'"* (12.310)

Sarpedon recognizes that the entire structure of his society, the only one available to him and Glaukos, rests on the fighting code. He is a product of that society, proud of his position in it and willing to live up to its personal and social ideals. However much he might prefer a life where he did not have to die in battle, he does not question what the code requires of him. The attractions of life at home do not tempt him to waver, for the quality of his life and his value depend upon "the main thing." In this famous speech Sarpedon confirms what we have already repeatedly observed, especially in the conduct of Diomedes in the opening books, the standard of normal behaviour which the group imposes on the warrior-leaders and which they willingly accept.

The *Iliad* makes clear, however, that this faith in the warrior code, although common to all Iliadic leaders, is in reality a tense affirmation of a sometimes fragile order, and that close under the surface of this tough creed lurks the chaos of a world from which any sense of social meaning has disappeared. Agamemnon's apparent denial of the tradi-tional code precipitates an instant disintegration of the social order (2.143), and the structure of the group, apparently so solid and ancient, immediately turns into chaos. On a more individual level, just before his final battle with Akhilleus, Hektor's loss of faith in the warrior code which he has followed all his life, as we shall see in Chapter 6, instantly causes him to lose control of himself in an absurd panic. In these mo-ments we recognize that the heroic code, like all significant systems of belief, is not a complacent faith in comforting axioms but a challenging, tense, and sometimes vulnerable means of creating worthy purpose in human endeavour, where without such faith life would become meaning-less.

The group code establishes certain conventions in the fighting. Even the fiercest combat, for all the animal frenzy it unleashes, follows certain rules (except for Akhilleus' *aristeia*, which falls outside the norm). The warrior often declares himself to his foe, announcing his worth by listing his past victories and his famous ancestors. The combat is almost in-variably a personal one, involving two named warriors, and, with leaders of the highest worth, it takes place at close quarters (hence, the contempt which spearmen sometimes express for archers). When a warrior falls, another takes his place, seeking to recover the body and to prevent the enemy from winning the weapons and armour of the dead man. Losing the fallen comrade and his gear to the opponent brings dishonour to the group. Frequently, a warrior will gloat over an enemy he has killed or will mock a spear thrown awry. A defeated warrior may offer ransom, and certain characters in the epic have in earlier times escaped death in this way. The victor makes the decision, however, and in the battles around Troy he customarily refuses the offer. In some instances, a war-rior may decline to fight, as Diomedes does with Glaukos, on the ground that he and his family enjoy a special relationship with the opponent (6.215). The heroic code thus makes very specific demands, and each leader knows what he must do in any particular situation.

It is important to note that the code does not demand suicidal bravery; under certain conditions a warrior may strategically withdraw from a fight against impossible odds or against an opponent whom a god is obviously favoring.

> *"Friends,*
> *all we can do is marvel at Prince Hektor.*
> *What a spearman he is, and what a fighter!*
> *One of the gods goes with him everywhere*
> *to shield him from a mortal wound. Look! there,*
> *beside him--Arês in disguise!*
>
> *Give ground*
> *slowly; keep your faces toward the Trojans.*
> *No good pitting ourselves against the gods."* *(5.601)*

To run from the battlefield brings dishonour, but an orderly retreat, with one's face still before the enemy, when the situation requires, makes perfect sense. No normal man need fight against the heavenly powers. The only significant inner debate the Iliadic warrior experiences is whether to stay at his post or move back; in such situations he must weigh the demands of the group against the power of the forces facing him. Occasionally, as in the above example, he invokes the gods to justify a retreat; at other times, his sense of personal honour keeps him where he is.

> *"Here is trouble.*
> *What will become of me? A black day, this,*
> *if I show fear and run before this crowd;*
> *but worse if I am captured, being alone.*
> *Zeus routed all the rest of the Danääns.*
> *But why this bandying inward words, my friend?*
> *Cowards are men who leave the front in war.*
> *The man who will be worth respect in battle*
> *holds on, whether he's hit or hits another."* *(11.404)*

In this case, Odysseus determines that he has more to lose by retreating than by staying, so he fights on. A few moments later, he is wounded (11.435) and retires with honour from the battle, for the code does not require injured parties to remain in the front lines. The heroic code, in other words, is a shared acceptance of certain unwritten rules, flexible enough to permit a limited range of different options but firm enough in each warrior's mind, so that he does not have to deliberate at length about what he must do.

If the quest for status in war establishes the group's shared values and channels the fighting energies of the community in a single direction, the desire to avoid a loss of status makes doubly sure that no one strays from the norm. For the greatest harm that can befall the warrior is shame, the community's public recognition that he has let the group down. The initial argument between Akhilleus and Agamemnon arises over a question of status and shame. Briseis herself has relatively little intrinsic importance; what matters above all is the recognition of worth which possession of her confers and the shame which will come with a public loss of the value she represents. In openly depriving Akhilleus of a military honour, Agamemnon shames Akhilleus so much that the latter abandons the fighting. The personal insult greatly outweighs all considerations of the common cause. No one questions the appropriateness of Akhilleus's actions; the Akhaians try to persuade him to return by appealing to the code, because they need him and his troops, but they never deny that Agamemnon has acted improperly. Later, of course, Agamemnon attempts to win Akhilleus back with munificent gifts which would make up many times over for what Akhilleus lost in the original quarrel. The fact that Akhilleus is not willing to accept his commander's reparations, as we shall see in Chapter 6, indicates just how far in his isolation he has moved from the normal standards of the community.

Throughout the poem we witness repeatedly the warriors' preoccupation with avoiding shame. When Nestor wishes the Akhaians to volunteer to fight Hektor, obviously an unwelcome assignment, which no one is immediately eager to carry out, he so shames his colleagues, characteristically by recalling his past exploits, that several leaders quickly step forward (7.124). As more than one commentator has pointed out, the familiar Greek word *nemesis*, which we associate with divine retribution, a principle of cosmic justice, in the *Iliad* means shame, the social punishment for failing to satisfy the demands of the group. And *nemesis* in this sense exercises a decisive control over the group: "the strongest moral force which Homeric man knows is not fear of god, but respect for public opinion. . . ." (Dodds 18). Just how powerful this can be we witness near the climax of the final battle between Hektor and Akhilleus, in the former's inner debate about whether to fight or to seek the security of the city immediately at his back.

> *"Here I am badly caught. If I take cover,*
> *slipping inside the gate and wall, the first*
> *to accuse me for it will be Poulydamas,*
> *he who told me I should lead the Trojans*
> *back to the city on that cursed night*
> *Akhilleus joined the battle. No, I would not,*
> *would not, wiser though it would have been.*
> *Now troops have perished for my foolish pride,*
> *I am ashamed to face townsmen and women.*
> *Someone inferior to me may say:*
> *'He kept his pride and lost his men, this Hektor!'*
> *So it will go. Better, when that time comes,*
> *that I appear as he who killed Akhilleus*

65

> *man to man, or else that I went down*
> *fighting him to the end before the city."* *(22.99)*

One should not remove this speech from its dramatic context. Hektor has every possible reason to return inside the city. He stands alone with nowhere else to go and has just witnessed a calamitous rout of his troops. Hektor's aged parents, Priam and Hekabe, have made the most urgent and pathetic pleas for his return, begging him to put consideration for his family, for the welfare of the citizens, who need Hektor's leadership, and for the safety of Troy before anything else. None of their moving eloquence can overcome Hektor's desire to avoid the shame he will encounter. Moreover, we have seen Hektor as a loving husband and father, so we understand what he risks in his refusal to return into the city. His fear of *nemesis* outweighs all these considerations. For him, as for all the warriors, death is preferable to dishonour.

This incident raises the question of the relationship between shame and the actions caused by divine interference. If Agamemnon can invoke the goddess Folly to escape the shame his countrymen might direct against him for his treatment of Akhilleus, why cannot Hektor do the same here? There is no absolutely clear answer to that, except to note that shame applies to those errors which fall inside the sphere of normal activity, that is, to the personal lapses from habitual behaviour. The appeal to divine interference applies only to the extraordinary departures from the norm. Hektor will here be shamed because, in the course of a normal battle, he has pushed his quest for fame too far, violating the prudence that warriors sometimes require and overlooking the urgent advice of his comrade Poulydamas. Moreover, if he refuses to face Akhilleus, he will contravene the most basic tenet of the heroic code: personal courage in hand-to-hand combat. He will be running away from an encounter that many other Trojans, lesser men than he, have already had the courage to undertake. Hektor can hardly refuse, in the name of prudence or divine interference, to risk his life, as they did.

We gain some insight into the relationship between *nemesis* and prudence in the debate between Nestor and Diomedes in Book Eight. In the midst of the battle, Nestor urges retreat, citing the usual reason:

> *"Give way, now; get the team to pull us out!*
> *Do you not realize that power from Zeus*
> *is being denied you? Glory goes today*
> *to Hektor, by favor of the son of Krónos.*
> *Another day he may bestow it on us*
> *if he only will. No man defends himself*
> *against the mind of Zeus--even the ruggedest*
> *of champions. His power is beyond us."* *(8.139)*

Diomedes, less experienced than Nestor, has his doubts about what people will think if he retreats. He has no desire to call his reputation into question.

> *"All that you say is right enough, old man.*
> *But here's atrocious pain low in my chest*
> *about my heart, when I imagine Hektor*
> *among the Trojans telling them one day:*
> *'Diomêdês made for the ships with me behind him!'*
> *That's the way he'll put it. May broad earth*
> *yawn for me then and hide me!"* (8.146)

Nestor reminds Diomedes that, having done his best, he has nothing to fear from later talk of disgrace.

> *"Ai, Diomêdês, keep your head, what talk!*
> *Even if Hektor calls you a coward*
> *he cannot make them think so, Trojans or Dardans,*
> *no, nor the Trojan soldiers' wives who saw*
> *their fine men in the dust, dead at your hands!"* (8.152)

The exchange clarifies the code somewhat. We must recognize that the commitment to honour has its limits. One does not challenge the gods, and they must be operating on the other side, if one has done one's best and finds the battle going the wrong way. But Hektor stranded outside the gates of Troy does not have this option. Akhilleus is only one man, and Hektor has not faced him squarely yet. The code requires that Hektor stand. In escaping this responsibility by returning inside, Hektor would be contravening the ethic which has made him, according to Sarpedon's observations to Glaukos, the most honored of the Trojans.

II

As he does with all aspects of the war, Homer shows us another side of the warrior code, how the demands of the group expose the ironic contradictions of combat. For if the heroic code inspires men with a sense of belonging and with a constant striving for excellence in a hazardous enterprise which demands the utmost in skill, loyalty, and courage, at the same time it requires men to stifle any latent desire to answer natural impulses which do not meet the often harsh, narrow rules of the group. When Menelaos, for example, is moved to spare the life of a defeated Trojan, Agamemnon points out in the most brutal terms that this battle has no room for human mercy.

> *"Oh, Meneláos,*
> *once in our hands not one should squirm away*
> *from death's hard fall! No fugitive, not even*
> *the manchild carried in a woman's belly!*
> *Let them all without distinction perish,*
> *every last man of Ilion,*
> *without a tear, without a trace!"*
>
> *Implacably*
> *thus he recalled his brother's mind to duty.... (6.57)*

And so Adrestos is slaughtered, for all his moving plea to Menelaos. Duty to the group does not permit the individual to answer personal feelings if they move beyond the limit set for appropriate behaviour on the battlefield, and in this instance that rule does not include sparing anyone for ransom or any other reason. Again and again, Homer places the killing of an individual warrior in the immediate context of an absent family, thus reminding us what the noble code costs, so that we are always aware of the ironic shadows cast by the quest for glory and a high status in the fighting group. Thus, the human potential of each man, although wonderfully realized in some respects, is also enormously limited. The rules which establish human value and dignity also annihilate the bearer of value ("his own courage kills him" 12.45), turning him into inert food for carrion.

The ironic combination of supreme human value and utter destruction of the individual who displays it manifests itself particularly in the final goal which the warrior sets himself. For the highest status he can achieve comes in the glorious memory of his famous deeds. Time will inevitably bring about his death in battle, but through his heroic fame his importance can live on in his family and community. The Iliadic leader seeks as the highest achievement of his harsh life not peaceful happiness or longevity or riches, but enduring fame (Dodds 17). Hence, the importance of the appropriate funeral ceremonies: the greater the hero, the more important the group recognition around the corpse. The ghost of Patroklos invokes the need for burial rites in order to pass the gates of Death, but the most important function of the rituals is to celebrate the memory of the dead hero, to make sure that his life will not be forgotten. In the extended ceremonies for Patroklos, which Akhilleus recognizes as a prefiguring of his own funeral, the most important task he gives the Akhaians is the construction of a suitably prominent and enduring memorial to Patroklos and himself.

> *"Then we'll pack his bones in a golden urn*
> *with sheepfat in a double fold, to keep*
> *until I too go hid in undergloom.*

> *No heavy labor at a heavy tomb*
> *I ask--only a fitting one; in due course*
> *build it wide and high, you who are left*
> *behind me in the long ships of the oarsmen." (23.243)*

When Hektor addresses both Trojans and Akhaians on the proper treatment of the corpse of a fallen warrior, he defines clearly the greatest glory he can imagine by killing his fellow men: the immortal reputation he will have once he too has perished.

> *"Akhaians there may give him funeral*
> *and heap a mound for him by Hellê's water.*
> *One day a man on shipboard, sailing by*
> *on the winedark sea, will point landward and say:*
> *'There is the death-mound of an ancient man,*
> *a hero who fought Hektor and was slain.'*
> *Someone will say that someday. And the honor*
> *won by me here will never pass away." (7.85)*

At the very moment he realizes that he is about to die, Hektor confirms the faith that has guided his whole life: he must go down fighting "in some action memorable to men in days to come" (22.305).

In this ceaseless striving for the immortality enshrined in a famous memory, the family has an important role to play. The warrior's parents matter because they, in part, establish his value to his peers and set a standard which he must live up to. He carries out his duties to them and defines his own worth by recalling their deeds. The warrior's children matter just as much because they will, in a similar manner, keep alive the great man's fame and thus guarantee the memory of his actions. For the same reason, Helen offers as the only justification for the terrible suffering ("all of misery, given by Zeus") the immortality they will attain through future artistic celebrations of their exploits: "that we may live in song for men to come" (6.357). The heroic code thus channels the vital energies of the heroes into the paradoxical search through killing and self-annihilation in war for something that will transcend time and fate. The warrior becomes most truly famous only when he has perished.

> What [Homer] exalts and sanctifies is not the triumph of victorious force but man's energy in misfortune, the dead warrior's beauty, the glory of the sacrificed hero, the song of the poet in times to come--whatever defies fatality and rises superior to it, even in defeat. (Bespaloff 79)

No matter how paradoxical the ironies of the heroic code, the warrior's adherence to it is unambiguous. None of the leaders directs at the group ethic any overt criticism, and they can be very severe on a colleague who fails to live up to its demands, as Diomedes, not one of the most senior officers, shows when he criticises his superior, the commander-in-chief (9.32). Again and again, the reader sees in their actions, ambitions, and beliefs the complex irony of their lives; the warriors, however, accept their situation without questioning it. Akhilleus, of course, becomes a special case. He is the tragic hero of the *Iliad* because he moves outside the group and from this position can achieve a different perspective upon the code and then, in his climactic *aristeia*, discover for himself the inescapably self-destructive contradictions at the heart of it. But for the normal warrior-leader, like Diomedes, Odysseus, Aias, Sarpedon, and Idomeneus, the road to fame always remains firmly inside the parameters set by the shared heroic code, and he thus remains unaware of the complexity of the experience in which he plays an integral part.

The contradictory limitations of the heroic code become even more evident to the reader, however, when he examines the life in Iliadic society of the non-combatants: the women, children, and old men. Obviously these groups cannot compete for status in battle, unless, like Nestor, they can remain in the front lines, and so they must derive their sense of worth from their relationship to a warrior as part of his identity. In a line quoted earlier, Nestor urges his men to "remember children and wives, possessions, and your parents" (15.662). The ambiguity in "possessions" reminds us that these non-combatants nearest and dearest the warrior have no intrinsic value as human beings, or if they do, it is far outweighed by their contribution to the warrior's standing among his peers. An interesting reminder of the worth of women in the society comes when we learn that the first prize for the wrestling match is "a fire-straddling tripod valued at twelve oxen" (23.702) and the second prize is "a woman versatile at crafts, whose value was four oxen" (23.704). The warrior needs a tripod to clean up after the battle; a woman well trained in artistic skills has far less use.[1] Similarly, Agamemnon offers Teukros as a fitting reward "a tripod or a team with car, or else a woman who will sleep with you" (8.290). In the *Iliad*, the fact of war shapes human values, and those who cannot contribute as warriors usually have a low rank. In the *Odyssey*, by contrast, women, and especially those gifted in art, music, and domestic life, occupy a place of high esteem. For similar reasons, old men in the *Iliad* generally count for little if their days of fighting have passed; they have become "like cicadas in dry summer" (3.151), strong only in their talking. Even Priam, the ruler of Troy, acknowledges the pathetic weakness of the old (22.71).

---

1 Some readers may object here that the woman in question is obviously a slave and therefore, by definition, a possession with a market value. She is still, however, a woman and a skilled artist, at that. It is not insignificant that she and her talent are worth less here than a common functional military object. Another woman, "a girl adept at gentle handicraft", is part of the first prize in the chariot races (23.263).

The ironic consequences of the warrior code emerge also in the most intimate domestic scene of the epic, the meeting of Hektor, Andromakhe, and Astyanax in Book Six. In response to Andromakhe's lament for the slaughter of her family in war and a plea to her one remaining protector to refrain from battle, Hektor delineates for us his vision of the heroic code, the paradoxical way of life which compels him to fight on.

> *"Lady, these many things beset my mind*
> *no less than yours. But I should die of shame*
> *before our Trojan men and noblewomen*
> *if like a coward I avoided battle,*
> *nor am I moved to. Long ago I learned*
> *how to be brave, how to go forward always*
> *and to contend for honor, Father's and mine.*
> *Honor--for in my heart and soul I know*
> *a day will come when ancient Ilion falls,*
> *when Priam and the folk of Priam perish."* (6.441)

But this potentially radical insight into the ambiguous nature of war--all the more significant because we know Akhilleus will soon claim Hektor as another victim--does not lead Hektor to criticize the heroic code. So devoted is he to the warrior life that, in imagining the disasters which will overtake the city, he acknowledges that the most painful thought of all is the knowledge that, even though he will have died, his name will be shamed by the public humiliation of Andromakhe, "the wife of Hektor, who fought best of Trojan horsemen when they fought at Troy" (6.460). His priority here echoes the reaction of Agamemnon earlier when he witnesses his brother's wound. For all his fraternal concern, Agamemnon's major worry is how his reputation will suffer if Menelaos dies (4.155). The intensely egoistic striving which the warrior code fosters obviously inhibits much concern for the welfare of others for their own sakes.

Then Hektor reaches for his son. The child, understandably terrified by the metallic figure of the armed warrior, wails in distress. In one of the most intimate domestic reactions in the entire poem, both the parents find the child's behaviour mildly comical, and together, in unison, they laugh. The mutual amusement at the cries of their baby son is quite an understandable reaction, but even here the affection of the moment has its complexities. For Hektor armed, a man transformed into a metallic apparition, is a fearsome sight, and the child's crying a natural response to a frightening vision. But to those whose life is defined by the heroic code, both Hektor and Andromakhe, the infant's distress is a source of amusement. Without seeing in this famous scene ominously

71

harsh ambiguities, we can still recognize the subtle ironies at work in that affectionate laughter, which stems, in part, from the parents' complete acceptance of the normality of war and their lack of awareness of any alternative. Moments later, in looking lovingly at his baby son, Hektor's hopes for the future confirm just how incapable he is of fully understanding the culture which has destroyed and will destroy so much human life, including his own.

> "O Zeus
> and all immortals, may this child, my son,
> become like me a prince among the Trojans.
> Let him be strong and brave and rule in power
> at Ilion; then someday men will say
> 'This fellow is far better than his father!'
> seeing him home from war, and in his arms
> the bloodstained gear of some tall warrior slain--
> making his mother proud." (6.476)

The scene present quite impartially the ironies of the warrior's life. Hektor and Andromakhe understand slaughter; they have seen and lamented its consequences, and they know it will overtake them and their fellows. Yet the only ambition they have for their son is a successful participation in the process that has exterminated or will soon exterminate every one of his immediate ancestors. One critic has suggested that Homer in this scene "dramatizes the pain of the warrior's role, of the man who, on behalf of his family, must leave his family, so that his very defense of them becomes a betrayal" (Redfield 123); another sees here that "Hektor's loyalties are divided" (Schein 174). But Hektor's proud, unambiguous ambitions for himself and Astyanax reveal no conscious confusion on his part. However much Andromakhe weeps for the killing of her family and whatever Hektor's concerns about the future, neither of them pushes the emotional attitude to the point where it raises any conscious criticism of the heroic way of life, in which their faith remains unswerving. The irony in the scene is all the more eloquent because of the genuine love we feel Hektor and Andromakhe have for each other and for their son and because we know what will happen to them soon enough. These are not unfeeling, ignorant, callous people, but a noble, loving, and sympathetic family. That they should so obviously remain uncritical of the destructive ironies of their life reminds the reader all the more vividly of the complexity of the picture of human existence which Homer is developing. Readers familiar with the well-known fate of Astyanax (flung from the walls of Troy by the conquering Akhaians) will see in Hektor's proud hopes an even stronger sense of the narrow limits the heroic code places on human understanding.

The way in which Hektor's and Andromakhe's loving laughter directs a critical insight into the adequacy of the heroic code brings to mind other moments in the poem where the shared intimacy of mutual laughter, in the midst of affectionate comradeship, reveals wide ironic overtones. Book Ten, for example, in which Diomedes and Odysseus carry out a daring and extraordinarily bloody raid against the Trojans, an episode which Homer describes so as to evoke the utmost pathos and revulsion against slaughter, concludes with general laughter at the carnage.

> "Diomêdês killed
> their master and a dozen fellow officers.
> A thirteenth man, a scout, abaft the ships
> we executed: Hektor and his peers
> had sent him forward to observe the army."

> Down through the moat he drove the horses now
> and laughed a rumbling laugh. Along with him
> the others crossed, exulting. (10.559)

In the laughter of Odysseus and his comrades we recognize a natural reaction, but the reminder of the pathetic, brutal deaths we have witnessed, the slaughter of sleeping soldiers and a helpless captive, qualifies our assent to the response. According to the warrior code, Odysseus and Diomedes have fared well and are fully entitled to gloat. What in the scale of human values, we may wonder, has that exultation cost? Homer provides no clear answer, but he makes us appreciate the complexity of the issue.

The most celebrated moment of general human laughter in the *Iliad* occurs in the famous episode with Thersites in Book Two. Here we must not let the literary descendants of the man, especially Shakespeare's version of him, conceal what he really says. For Thersites's objection to the entire enterprise, the only speech we have from a common soldier, merits close attention.

> "Agamémnon!
> What have you got to groan about? What more
> can you gape after? Bronze fills all your huts,
> bronze and the hottest girls--we hand them over
> to you, you first, when any stronghold falls.
> Or is it gold you lack? A Trojan father
> will bring you gold and ransom for his boy--
> though I--or some poor footsoldier like myself--
> roped the prisoner in.
>
> Or a new woman

73

to lie with, couple with, keep stowed away
for private use--is that your heart's desire?
You send us back to bloody war for that?
Comrades! Are you women of Akhaia?
I say we pull away for home, and leave him
here on the beach to lay his captive girls!
Let him find out if we troops are dispensable
when he loses us!" (2.225)

The language may be colloquially rough, and Thersites "the most ob-
noxious rogue who went to Troy," but the speech calls into question the
basic assumptions of the group in a manner unlike anything else in the
poem. For Thersites is essentially challenging the value of the warrior
code. He directs at it what we might call (stretching things a bit) a rational, humanistic and democratic objection: Look here, this war is not
fair to me and my fellow common soldiers, so why don't we all stop fighting and go home? In his reply to Thersites, Odysseus does not even meet
the objection on its own terms; instead he berates Thersites with invec-
tive and attacks him physically until Thersites whimpers and cowers away
from the blows. The soldiers then laugh at the sight of the "poisonous
clown" in pain. The reaction confirms their adherence to the communal
ethic. But the reader, standing outside the heroic code, sees the ironic
implication of "noble" Odysseus' answer. In this way of life, there is no
place for Thersites' criteria; to admit them would be to undermine the
entire social fabric. Odysseus does not here display his legendary
duplicity, concealing his appreciation for Thersites' thinking behind a
necessary stratagem. As an orthodox representative warrior-leader who
subscribes to the conventional beliefs in warfare, Odysseus does not even
comprehend what Thersites means. He sees the objection as an insult
to Agamemnon's status and a violation of the ethical norms, that is, as
heresy (which it is), and he acts accordingly.[2] The laughter his behaviour
prompts from the soldiers is, once again, double edged.

In his play *Comedians*, Trevor Griffiths calls attention to two common forms of the joke. The first confirms people's existing attitudes: the

---

2   Some commentators have drawn comparisons between Thersites' objection and the
    initial outbursts of Akhilleus. So, for example, Whitman observes: "Few things are
    more subtle in the Iliad than the way in which this 'good-for-nothing,' the social and
    physical antitype of Achilles, reiterates the resentment of the hero. . . " (161). The
    significant differences between the two episodes, however, should not be overlooked.
    Akhilleus' objection comes from a man who believes in the code; his faith in it fuels
    his anger at the loss of status, and his accusations, made in extreme fury, are not
    altogether justified, as we shall see in Chapter 6. Thersites' objection, on the other
    hand, comes from someone outside the warrior code who is rejecting it because it is
    inherently unfair to those who must risk the dangers without the concomitant rewards.

laughter expresses a group response to what its members do not want to face, and it thus releases any tension a challenge to orthodoxy might create and, in the process, reinforces the limitations in the value system of the group. The second form of joke "has to do more than release tension, it has to *liberate* the will and the desire, it has to *change the situation*" (20). Such laughter educates its audience into a new awareness of normality. The laughter of the men in the *Iliad*, and the epic does not contain very much, obviously belongs in the first category. It operates as a harsh confirmation of the community's standards at the expense of anyone or anything which might threaten to open a momentary breach in the closed awareness of the group, and it thus possesses none of the educating influence of the laughter common in mature comedies, which transforms the individual's awareness of himself, leaving him changed in some small but important way. Thus, in the *Iliad* the warrior's sense of humour displays a characteristically complex irony, of which he remains quite unaware.[3]

It might be interesting to observe, in this connection, that the form of laughter very commonly associated with modern war fictions, and therefore the war humour with which we are most familiar, is wholly absent from the *Iliad*: that laughter which arises from the sense of war as an absurd farce, of the sort developed, for example, in *Catch-22*, *M.A.S.H.*, or *Gravity's Rainbow*. Such humour emerges as a last-ditch protection against the final surrender of a collapsing faith, a stylish and often very desperate affirmation of something in the face of the total absurdity of human existence. The laughter in the *Iliad*, however, always serves to confirm, roughly and effectively, the traditional system of belief. We, as readers, do not share the joke, for we are not meant to, but we do see how the communal merriment exposes the limitations of that faith, reminding us again that in its endorsement of human values, the heroic code necessarily excludes many possibilities for a more all-encompassing vision of human potential.

3 The funny story Hephaistos tells against himself to resolve a potentially dangerous domestic scene is another matter (1.590). The incident points out to us that the rich joys of the second type of comedy, which enables man to deal with strife through wit rather than through egoistic confrontation, are available only on Olympos, for no warrior can ever act as Hephaistos does here to "change the situation." Zeus typically acts as the warriors do; his favorite laughter is a roar of glee at other people's expense.

CHAPTER 5

Arms and the Men

Invisibly, the mechanism sings.
It sings. It sings like a six-ton flute:
east, west, always the same
note stuck in the rivetless throat.

And yet, a song as intricate
as any composition by Varèse,
and seeming, for the moment, still
more beautiful, because,

to us, more deadly.
Therefore purer, more
private, more familiar,
more readily feared, or desired:

a dark beauty with a steel sheen,
caught in the cocked
mind's eye and brought
down with an extension of the hand.

(Robert Bringhurst, "The Beauty of the Weapons")

I

In depicting the world of the heroes in the *Iliad*, Homer pays special attention to the objects of war, the material possessions inextricably linked to the demands of the warrior's daily occupation. And just as we derive significant insight into any culture by examining the artifacts which the people most value, so in the *Iliad* we are constantly discovering the ironies of war in the articles which the fighting men use. Not surprisingly, then, if we scrutinize closely the material world in the epic we find that the cultural values symbolized by this civilization's prized objects evoke the same contradictory responses as the fighting and the religious and social systems with which the men comprehend themselves and their society.

We notice from the start that the material world of the *Iliad* is, in many respects, extraordinarily narrow. Almost every object in the poem has a practical use in the war, and objects with no direct military function or with no bearing on the warrior's status as a fighting man count for very little or do not merit any detailed attention. A copper cauldron, for example, has a value three times that of a woman skilled in crafts, because the soldier needs a good cauldron in the field; he does not require domestic fine arts. Readers who come to the *Iliad* directly from the *Odyssey*, or vice versa, often remark upon the considerable difference in texture between the two poems. Much of that sense comes from the way in which the *Odyssey* constantly celebrates the beauties of architecture, gardens, furniture, clothes, and other created objects and environments for their aesthetic value rather than for what they reveal about the status of the possessor; whereas, the world of the *Iliad* has little room for such a rich variety. In the world of peaceful, hospitable human civilization central to the *Odyssey*, the artistic magnificence of homes, like the rich beauty of even common domestic objects and the paradisal qualities of nature, brings into man's life a vitally important aesthetic pleasure. The world of the *Iliad*, by contrast, has no room for art except as it manifests itself in functional war gear or in objects pertinent to the war effort. The world of the *Odyssey* contains a wide variety of splendid articles that continually evoke from Odysseus a delight unconnected to any desire for status or to any particular function. And those responsible for producing such beauty deserve special praise. Hence, the importance in the *Odyssey* of women skilled in crafts, of musicians and dancers, and of all the artistically gifted. Women in this world occupy an honored place; to a large extent they create and maintain the institutions which bring joy, purpose, and value to human life. And artists like Demodokos, who would be quite useless on the battlefield, enjoy a special eminence in the social world of the royal court, a place which also celebrates the family and convivial hospitality. The *Iliad* also honours the creative skills of man, of course, but here the imaginative talent of the artist concerns itself almost exclusively with weapons of destruction. Women and the fine arts associated with them, like the wondrous beauties of natural scenery, have an insignificant intrinsic value by comparison.

In the *Iliad*, we find, for example, no marked celebration of the aesthetic magnificence of Troy. We learn that it is a rich, powerful, well-guarded city and that Priam's palace, "fair and still, made all of ashlar, with bright colonnades," contains "fifty rooms of polished stone" (6.242). But Homer spares us any further details, declining the opportunity to digress at length on anything not immediately relevant to warfare. He concentrates his attention rather on what matters most in this world: the battlefield exploits of the men who occupy the fifty rooms and the weapons that they and their enemies use to kill each other.[1] Nestor's humble field hut, an important military installation, merits as much attention as Priam's royal apartments. Similarly, the poem rarely offers us a glimpse of objects or activities in Troy which have no direct military significance, no matter how beautiful they may be. When Hektor visits the women in Paris's house (6.318), the ladies are engaged in "needlecraft and splendid weaving." But, however impressive the women's craft, Homer's description draws our attention emphatically to the really beautiful artistic creations in the scene: Hektor's spear, "eleven forearms long, whose bronze head shone before him in the air," and Paris' "magnificent cuirass and shield."

The non-military objects which do matter are those which play some part in the warrior's status or which maintain the central fighting ethic of the community. Helen's weaving in Book Three merits attention because the work depicts "many passages of arms by Trojan horsemen and Akhaians mailed in bronze--trials braved for her sake at the wargod's hands" (3.126). The gorgeous materials in Hekabe's wardrobe, one of the prizes of Paris' raid against Menelaos, come to our notice only because Hektor requires an appropriate war offering to Athena (6.289). Akhilleus has a wonderful "sweet harp of rich and delicate make--the crossbar set to hold the strings being silver" (9.186), and he sings in his isolation from the battle. More important than the artistic beauty of the instrument or the song, however, are the facts that the harp is a battle trophy and that the lyric celebrates ancient fighting heroes. The song of men destroying each other to the accompaniment of the instrument which Akhilleus has won by the immolation of a city brings him much joy. Beautiful music serves to maintain the spirit of the warrior. The moment provides a significant contrast to Odysseus's reaction in the *Odyssey* to the songs about Troy: there he finds the tales of battle desolating. The description of Nestor's cup in 11.632 provides one possible exception to this exclusive concentration upon functional war materials, and even here the author draws our attention to how drinking from the mag-

---

1   Schein disagrees on this point: "The beauty and sophistication of the architecture, combined with Homer's emphasis on the sleeping arrangements of Priam's children and their spouses, show Troy to be a center of civilized refinement and domestic decorum" (170). It strikes me that the magnificence of Troy and the importance of women are rather conspicuously absent from Homer's descriptions. The comment from Schein seems to be part of his continuing attempt to insist upon some important cultural difference between the opponents, between, that is, "the masculine society of the Greek army" and the society in Troy, which honours "the distinct role and sphere of women" (173), in the service of his reassuring vision of the war as a moralized combat.

nificent vessel proves Nestor's physical strength, so the notion of warrior status is not altogether absent.

In the same way, the *Iliad* pays relatively little attention to the daily needs of food or sleep. The meals are important chiefly as a preparation for battle or as part of a group ritual, maintaining the solidarity of the fighting units. The warriors do not take a delight in the feast for its own sake, as a joyous, social communion with friends. None of the cozy human warmth of the *Odyssey*, the emphasis on beautiful manners, fine dishes, wonderfully potent wine, musical entertainment, and warm beds--none of this exists in the *Iliad*. When we do sense something approaching that form of human pleasure, as in the scene of Nestor's entertaining his friends (11.618 ff.), the demands of war, this time in the form of Patroklos, quickly interrupt the social gathering. Perhaps the closest we come to such a feeling of the disinterested pleasure of social interaction, and the difference is still striking, occurs at the very end of Book Ten.

> *Wading into the sea, the men themselves*
> *splashed at their coats of sweat--shins, nape, and thighs--*
> *until the surf had washed it from their skin*
> *and they were cool again. Then out they came*
> *to take warm baths in polished tubs. Being bathed*
> *and rubbed with olive oil, the two sat down*
> *to take refreshment. From a full winebowl*
> *they dipped sweet wine and poured it to Athêna. (10.572)*

The picture celebrates the intense male comradeship which comes from sharing success in a hazardous enterprise. And we can sense the mutual joy in a daring victory for which sweet wine provides an appropriate libation and refreshment. But once again the stress falls on the war; the two friends are, after all, washing off the blood and sweat of slaughter. And the final reference to Athena, whom the two warriors are thanking for success, echoes a similar reference a few lines earlier which reminds us of the helpless victim: "Odysseus hung the bloodstained gear of Dolôn--pending a proper offering to Athêna" (10.570). The bathing and the refreshment, therefore, do not register as an entirely delightful and civilized social ritual designed to bring repose after a long day (as they would in the *Odyssey*); the impression is that Odysseus and Diomedes badly need a wash and some emotional relief to be ready for the next day's killing.

That part of material civilization in the *Iliad* which does have a preeminent importance is, naturally enough, the weapons of war. To own the most impressive armour, a spear which no other man can throw, or a large number of captured arms marks a man as a warrior of special merit. For example, a request for the loan of a spear provides Idomeneus an opportunity to proclaim his public worth and to indicate his priorities.

> *"Spears? All you desire,*
> *twenty-one spears, you'll find inside, arrayed*
> *against the bright wall of the entranceway--*
> *all Trojan; I win weapons from the dead.*
> *I do not hold with fighting at long range,*
> *therefore I have the spears, and shields as well,*
> *and helms as well, and bright-faced cuirasses." (13.260)*

Idomeneus values the spears (significantly he knows the exact total) and displays them prominently in his quarters because they possess a great value as practical weapons and as marks of his worth to his peers. And he does not hesitate to point out to Meriones that a warrior can only win spears from the enemy in hand-to-hand combat, in the fiercest fighting of all, the battle over the corpse of a fallen leader. And Meriones, for all the urgency of the battle situation, takes the time to respond to the implied challenge in Idomeneus' remarks by pointing out his own prowess manifested in the weapons he has in his quarters. In the *Iliad* we find no false modesty about possessions of war nor any careless indifference to those details which declare the status of the owner. Nor do we see any envious attitudes that deceitfully deny the value of some else's equipment. The leaders may argue about who owns the finest armour, but they agree on what constitutes fine armour and on the importance of having the best. The man who foolishly trades his good equipment for the inferior equipment of another, as Glaukos does with Diomedes, must have lost his wits (6.234).

This attitude to material things is neither pure covetousness nor an excessive desire for ostentatious displays of mere wealth. Possessions matter because they announce the warrior's status and are a public statement of his power. The sometimes vicious attitudes towards comrades in the funeral games, the hot tempers and almost suicidal tactics in the chariot race appearing quite incommensurate to what we might consider the intrinsic value of the prize, show just how much these men desire the objects that enhance their owner's public value. In a sense, we might even say that the warriors in the *Iliad* attack each other primarily because they wish to acquire more fine booty which will increase their reputation. Stripping an enemy for his weapons, even at great risk, is a cultural imperative, just as much an obligation as defending a fallen comrade from an enemy who wants to do the same. In the night foray of Diomedes and Odysseus, for example, the Argive pair eagerly kill thirteen defenseless sleeping Thracians to obtain enemy horses. Nothing in Homer's description of the event suggests glory in the slaughter, quite the reverse, and we get no sense that the horses will benefit the Argives materially in the battle. Ownership of the horses, however, marks Odysseus as a heroic man, favoured of the gods and therefore even more important among his peers. Moved by the same spirit, Hektor urges on his horses with an explanation of why the battle matters: it gives him an opportunity for more booty.

> *"Press the Akhaians hard, give all you have,*
> *and we may capture Nestor's shield whose fame*
> *has gone abroad to the sky's rim: all in gold*
> *they say it's plated, crossbars too. Then too*
> *remember the enameled cuirass worn*
> *by Diomêdês, crafted by Hêphaistos.*
> *If we can take these arms, I have a chance*
> *to drive the Akhaians aboard ship tonight!" (8.191)*

Hektor appears to want the spoils just as much as, if not more than, the victory. Nestor's shield matters, not because Hektor requires a superior weapon (the emphasis on gold, which symbolizes the social value of the shield, suggests that it would not be of much practical use in any case) but rather because the shield has a public reputation, a fame, which Hektor will acquire if he can get it in for his collection.

The detail with which Homer describes many of the weapons, especially his stress on the artistry in their construction, brings out the cultural worth of these objects and invariably evokes once more the ironic paradox at the heart of the warrior's civilization. The passage introducing the reader to the bow of Pandaros is a well-known example.

> *He uncased*
> *his bow of polished horn--horn of an ibex*
> *that he had killed one day with a chest shot*
> *upon a high crag; waiting under cover,*
> *he shot it through the ribs and knocked it over--*
> *horns, together, a good four feet in length.*
> *He cut and fitted these, mortised them tight,*
> *polished the bow, and capped the tips with gold. (4.105)*

One notices here, as in other such descriptions of particular weapons, the emphasis on the process of creating the object. The bow is the product of human resourcefulness, courage, patience, and skill, a tribute to an energetic and remarkable artistic creativity which transforms nature into something both functional and beautiful. The weapon marks the quality of Pandaros as a gifted individual who can meet the dangers of the mountains, the difficulty of the shot, and the challenge of the material to create something uniquely his. Pandaros does not just decorate the weapon with gold; the rich quality of the bow is an essential part of its artistic and practical excellence. Without the gold tip, the weapon would be missing an essential part, the protection where the bowstring is attached to the bow. At the same time, however, the magnificent bow is playing its part in a cruel, deadly enterprise. Immediately before the description we are told what Pandaros is about to do with the remarkable weapon (break the truce and thus cause the fighting to recommence), and immediately after the lines quoted above, we are reminded what function the unique work of art serves: it launches feathered arrows "never frayed, but keen with waves of pain to darken vision." The gods have given Pandaros his skill, and nature provides him with the materials. He dedicates his admirable creative energies to fashioning a beautiful and valued object which carries out a deadly function.

To separate value and function in this manner is perhaps misleading, since the *Iliad* always associates value, beauty, and function in an inextricable combination. For weapons, like human beings, display their excellence, their unique value, only in action or in potential for action. This notion of excellence (of *arete*, a word very difficult to render exactly in translation) includes the sense that worth depends on the proper fulfillment of the function for which the agent, man or material object, was made. For something to have value, it must fulfil its *arete*; it must, that is, realize as completely as possible in action the specific virtues for which it exists. In the *Iliad* a man's *arete* displays itself only in the fighting; similarly an object's *arete* depends upon its contributions to the war. And just as none of the warrior heroes is ugly, for the fighting which proves his excellence makes him beautiful (Thersites, who wants to abandon the fight, is the only physically ugly man mentioned in the poem), so the weapons of war are beautiful; their deadly potential makes them so.

This notion that the excellence of the weapon, like the merit of its owner, depends not just on its appearance but also on its performance creates those curious moments in the poem when the weapons acquire a vital life of their own.

> *Spears thrown by brawny hands*
> *at times would stick in his great shield; the rest*
> *stood fixed midway in earth before they reached*
> *the white flesh they were famished for. (11.571)*

> *then from bold men's hands*
> *a rain of spears came. Some stuck fast in agile*
> *fighters' bodies; many between the ranks*
> *fell short of the white flesh and stood a-quiver,*
> *fixed in earth, still craving to be sated. (15.314)*

The spear robbed of its "white flesh" has not fulfilled its function; its *arete* has been violated. The last quiverings of the spear which has not found a human target, like the final death throes of the defeated warrior, call to our attention that grim paradox central to the poem: in this warfare creative fulfillment, the proper realization of one's excellence, can only come through the successful destruction of life.

The paradoxical union of artistic beauty and destructive function runs throughout the *Iliad*. Even in the most unlikely places we find Homer insisting on the mysterious beauty of war, not only in the descriptions of weapons but also, more curiously, in the images of wounds.

> *Then dark blood rippled in a clouding stain*
> *down from the wound, as when a Mêionian*
> *or a Karian woman dyes clear ivory*
> *to be the cheekpiece of a chariot team.*
> *Though horseman after horseman longs to carry it,*
> *the artifact lies in a storeroom, kept*
> *for a great lord, a splendour doubly prized—*
> *his team's adornment and his driver's glory.*
> *So, Meneláos, were your ivory thighs*
> *dyed and suffused with running blood, your well-made*
> *shins and ankles, too. (4.140)*

The comparison here between the peaceful work of famous artists and the wound of Menelaos, one of the most remarkable similes in the poem, comes as a surprise. Wounds, too, like deadly bows, can bring a momentary beauty into the bloody work. This is not a strained rhetorical celebration of bloodshed (of the sort we read about in Marlowe's *Tamburlaine*, for example), but an impersonal fact of warrior life. In this way, Homer is always forcing us to confront the unexpected, to pause in the midst of the hectic fighting to dwell upon an image which calls to our attention the ambiguous character of war: the beauty amid the destruction. War summons up man's most admirable creative efforts in the service of the instruments of slaughter. Blood can be beautiful, but it comes from the bodies of the wounded and the dying. The severed head of a fallen hero, with the spear still in the eye-socket, the victor holds aloft "as one would lift a poppy" (14.499).

The most graphic image of the warrior armed depicts him in his chariot riding in glorious triumph over a sea of blood.

> *At this, he shook out reins*
> *to his glossy team with blowing manes, and used*
> *the cracking whip. And when they felt the lash,*
> *they drew the nimble chariot briskly on*
> *through Trojans and Akhaians, trampling shields*
> *and bodies of the dead. The axle-tree*
> *beneath was blood-bespattered; round the car*

the rails were spattered; from the horses' hooves
and from the wheel-rims blood flew up in spray. (11.531)

Hektor, Kebriones, and the chariot, the most complex product of man's unique creative skill, the union of animal force, artistically shaped material, and coordinated human control, here arise out of the earth and define the glory of the warrior in motion. This picture of the power of nature harnessed by the skill of man and yoked to a beautiful created object symbolizes the living warrior's most heroic pose. As Hektor moves nimbly and briskly, he presents to the world his glorious individuality, his full value as a human being, his *arete*. Significantly, Hektor's appearance here and elsewhere stresses how the beautiful artistic creativity of the man at war changes the human form. His physical nature he conceals behind shaped metal; he does not move across the earth in a natural human motion, but rides in a beautiful but destructive chariot. The image of Hektor in his glory, like the very similar picture of Akhilleus later in the poem, insists upon the full realization of heroic individuality by the denial of some important aspects of our common humanness. Moreover, the beautiful vision of man, animal, and machine grows out of the bloodshed which nurtures it and which will, in turn, transform the wonderful cultural achievement of chariot, armour, weapons, and men into a thing of bloody terror. The pursuit of glory takes place amid a shower of blood which the activity itself necessarily generates. The slaughter of men, which has given Hektor his lofty station, changes the green earth into a murky swamp of mud, bodies, weapons, and blood that will soon enough engulf Hektor himself and every other warrior in his turn. Sprung from the vital energies which arise spontaneously from the earth and returned in a mangled mess back into the earth, the Iliadic warrior lives for that brief moment when he can declare his individual glory in proud confidence, fully armed, a metallic work of art, still only a few feet from the ground, but moving superbly and reaching with his spear upward to the sky. The image stands out clearly, but its resonance reverberates as mysteriously as the eternal and violent rhythms of nature.

II

The physical objects in the *Iliad* can also derive their significance from the traditional cultural associations they embody. Since one of the important functions of art, especially in a society as conservative as the warrior group in the *Iliad*, is to enshrine and to transmit the established values of the past, not surprisingly the warrior's possessions, as well as defining his status among his peers, link him to the famous leaders of the past, even to the gods themselves. The helmet Meriones provides for

Odysseus (10.260) has come by a circuitous route from the military booty won by Autolykos, Odysseus's maternal grandfather, through a number of other people, and finally to Odysseus' ally from Crete. The object is obviously more than just a useful protection for the coming exploit; it has a cultural importance as well, which informs us that Odysseus is now participating in a traditional and universal activity, one which links him to a famous ancestor and to other warriors from distant lands. Sometimes the cultural associations of an important material possession can remind us of the continuing ironies of the traditional code. A well-known example is the royal sceptre of Agamemnon. Originally a product of Hephaistos' divine skill and a present to Zeus, it has passed from the father of the gods and men to Hermes, then to Pelops, from him to Atreus, then to Thyestes, and finally to Agamemnon. As part of Agamemnon's royal appearance in the assembly, the sceptre reminds every member of his audience of the conservative values on which their respect for the commander-in-chief's authority rests. For the reader who recognizes in the names the famous curse on the House of Atreus (since Pelops, Atreus, Thyestes, and Agamemnon are all principal characters in the most savage internecine feud in our culture), the sceptre acquires also an ominous sense of doom for the possessor, in the same way as does the armour of Akhilleus, which in the full story of the Trojan war destroys almost all those great heroes who wear it or seek to possess it: Patroklos, Hektor, Akhilleus, and Telamonian Aias.

This sense of the cultural importance of the beauty in the weapons emerges most clearly in the descriptions of the distinctive armour with which the heroes announce their individual human worth and at the same time conceal their frail bodies from the deadly perils of war. The passage in Book Eleven picturing Agamemnon's equipment declares the king's importance, for the cuirass is a royal gift from Lord Kinyres, and the rest so magnificent that even the gods thunder their approval. Everything in the outfit forms an essential part of the warrior's equipment, yet each piece also has a distinctive beauty: his shield is "a work of art for battle" and a terrifying reminder of the reality of death, "fire-eyed Gorgon's horrifying maw enclosed, with Rout and Terror flanking her" (11.36). Agamemnon's armour enables him to carry into battle not just a useful military protection or a declaration of his royal pre-eminence, but also an artistic expression of the greatest cultural achievements of his society. He goes into battle declaring to all in his person the full values of his civilization: personal courage, enormous individual authority, images of terrifying ferocity and artistic beauty. Agamemnon armed thus symbolizes both the most vital faith and the most admirable achievements of his people.

Most of us know enough about the history of weapons to recognize just how important the connection is between the soldier who destroys and the artist who creates. As Kant observed, the urge to warfare paradoxically stimulates the highest cultural achievements.[2] The Japanese samurai, for example, fought with a sword that was simultaneously one of the most efficient implements of destruction ever devised and an emblem of his culture, an object of surpassing beauty, which carried on it in the engraved poetry the emotional certainties basic to his creed. The blood of the slaughtered enemy flowed over the delicately etched verses. It would be difficult to find a practical cultural object anywhere that so clearly expresses the paradoxical aspirations of the warrior. Even today, our own personal response to the machinery of modern combat often indicates that we continue to find important cultural values in weapons, in the beautiful form and the deadly function wedded eternally in the lethal implement.[3]

Given the obvious cultural importance of the weapons in the *Iliad*, we recognize clearly the particular significance of the lengthy description of the divine armour of Akhilleus in Book Eighteen. In this section Homer gives us a vision central to the entire epic, and he does so by describing the weapons of the mightiest warrior of all. The god Hephaistos, the supreme artist, makes the shield for Akhilleus, who is about to push the heroic code to its limits and beyond. Before we witness the tragic *aristeia* of Akhilleus, however, we contemplate in the design of the shield the most complete single metaphor for the world of the *Iliad*. Whatever our response to Akhilleus may be as he launches his bloody revenge, we know his conduct grows out of the way of life his armour celebrates, for he carries the divine image of that life through all his remaining battles.

Hephaistos first emphasises in the design that the scenes on the shield take place within the context of the entire cosmos.

---

2 "On the cultural level hitherto attained war is an indispensable means of promoting culture; only when the perfect state is reached (god alone knows when) will peace be a blessing to us, indeed, only then will it be possible" (qtd in Ginsberg 52).
3 The popularity of modern war movies derives in large measure from the striking images they often provide of the beautiful and deadly machinery of battle. The most impressive and critically acclaimed scenes from Apocalypse Now, for example, are those of the helicopter gun-ships streaking in at dawn over the surf, with the music from Götterdämmerung blasting from the speakers. Similarly, the very opening image from Platoon, in which we see the huge military transport disgorge new recruits from its maw and swallow up body bags, speaks with a more eloquent intensity than anything else in the film. And who would pay any attention to Rambo without his M-16?

He pictured on it earth, heaven, and sea,
unwearied sun, moon waxing, all the stars
that heaven bears for garland: Plêïadês,
Hyadês, Oríôn in his might,
the Great Bear, too, that some have called the Wain,
pivoting there, attentive to Oríôn,
and unbathed ever in the Ocean stream. (18.483)

These first figures on the shield, like the very last ("all the might of the Ocean stream" 18.607) indicate that the human life depicted exists within the framework of the total universe. What does not appear on the shield is not part of life; what we see on the shield represents all the possibilities of life, realized in the perfection of divine art.

Then follow two scenes of civilized life. In the first, human beings celebrate weddings, music, dancing, and a peaceful and reasonable arbitration for murder through competitive performance in the law court. In the second scene, human life devotes itself to war--with Ares and Athena, as usual, prominent in the fray (significantly enough, the only Olympian deities on the shield). The latter picture evokes the full ironies of battle: the men "compact in bronze" kill and are killed under the rule of Strife and Uproar and the unpredictable "ghastly Fate" that arbitrarily wounds one man and not another. One notices at once the differences between the scenes. The most obvious contrast is that between the peaceful, creative, civilized life in the city, where men adjudicate even the most serious of crimes in a reasonable, controlled manner, and the hazardous, destructive enterprise of war beyond the walls. In the first scene the emphasis falls on everyone alike: the young men have an important role in the dancing; women move freely to join in the festivities; the old men occupy the important places as participants in the legal proceedings. In the second scene, the old men, women, and children can only stand on the wall keeping watch. The adult men--all the physically active mature men--have gone to war.

The juxtaposition of these two faces of civilization has an obvious importance. One does not find, however, any simple logical connection between them. For instance, the description of Hephaistos' design does not hint, as it might have done, that the second scene represents an action occasionally necessary in defense of the first. Such a possibility would suggest, of course, a more comforting view of war than we have witnessed in the poem, namely, that war does not have a pre-eminent place in man's affairs except as an essential but temporary undertaking in defense of civilization's more important values: marriage, peaceful celebration, and reasonable justice. The war scene rather represents a permanent feature of man's condition, an eternal part of the cosmic design. The contrasting images display two different worlds, each a divinely established aspect of man's lot, but significantly only one of them places any emphasis on the communal activity of mature, active, male adults. Nature may have two faces, and each scene belongs to the eternal pattern of the universe, but the design does not suggest that the two are rational alternatives. The picture impersonally evokes once again the sense that in the heavenly scheme, warfare is an inescapable fact of life.[4]

The pictures on the shield which follow the opening contrast again depict the different faces of nature. The earth provides for man the chance to plough, to harvest, and to enjoy fine wines and rich communal feasts. But the earth is equally home to the lions who live to gratify their carnivorous appetites. The divine artisan does not resolve the contradiction; he offers no proper synthesis of peaceful fertility and civilized control with the passionate and brutal frenzy in war, for there is no middle ground. To express fully the mysterious contradictions of life, man must rely on artistic inspiration. So the final human scene celebrates the "magical dancing"--an entire society rejoicing "spellbound" in man's imaginative power to translate the incomprehensible ambiguities of life into human beauty and joy in the coordinated rhythmic movement of the group. The reference to Daidalos invokes the spirit of the most famous human artist of all, the man who built the magical labyrinth around the destructive Minotaur and recalls for us the central paradox of human creativity linked to destruction. The shield here shows us a peaceful dance, but like the "dance of war" we have followed throughout the *Iliad*, it reminds us that the highest achievement we can aim for in a hostile world is a pattern of joyful physical movement, a rhythmic beauty that will last as long as men have the will to express themselves against the harsh irrationality of fate. As the artist-god gives shape to the metal, forming an object of eternal beauty, so men shape their lives, individually and collectively, to find meaning where without their efforts chaos would rule supreme. And that effort produces, by the most natural means, the dance of war.

Cedric Whitman quite rightly observes that the shield of Akhilleus functions as a metaphor and that we therefore waste our time trying to draw the exact picture or to unearth an identical artifact (126). Never-

---

4 Kenneth John Atchity sees in the symbolism of the divine shield a moral message preaching the evils of battle and the goodness of civil, peaceful strife. For him the shield is remarkable for its "didactic distinction" (185). This view is yet another example of the persistent critical habit of forcing onto Homer's fatalistic and irrational sense of war a moral scheme more comforting to modern sensibilities. See Chapter 7 for a fuller discussion of this and related matters.

theless, there is at least one suggestive archeological parallel to this famous description. Some years ago, in April 1975, an exhibition of ancient Scythian art opened in the Metropolitan Museum in New York City. This warrior culture in the seventh and sixth centuries produced some magnificent objects, recognizably similar to Iliadic art. Of one piece, the reviewer Robert Hughes observed:

> The centerpiece of the exhibition is, however, the 12-in.-wide gold pectoral dug from a kurgan or burial mound near the town of Ordzhonikidze in 1971. In the upper course we see domestic life: sheep, foals, calves, a pair of Scythians making a skin shirt. In the middle, vegetable nature: an exquisite frieze of curling tendrils and blossoms with tiny birds perching on them. And below, the goldsmith set forth the central myth of Scythian life: endless combat, unceasing subjugation of the weak by the strong--griffons attacking horses, feral cats killing deer. An entire world is summed up, with a sculptural intensity that Donatello could hardly have surpassed; and one cannot say whether ferocity or beauty prevails, or whether, for the Scythians, there was any difference between the two. (54)

Homer does not end the description of Akhilleus's armour with the evocative picture of the dancers and the surrounding boundaries of the universe. Before the end of the Book Eighteen, he brings the reader suddenly and prosaically back to the reality of the situation, by reminding us once again what this surpassingly beautiful work of art really is, namely, a practical necessity for the great warrior about to set forth on his destructive, glorious career. We thus recall that the creation of the greatest artistic work also serves the war; without the fighting, without Akhilleus's urge to battle, there would be no shield. Ironically, the most eloquent celebrations of peaceful life and artistic achievements occur only on this war implement. Homer thus reminds us that this war fosters a realization of the highest potential in the divine and human artistic imagination.

CHAPTER 6

The Iliad as a Tragedy:

The Warrior, the Victim, and the Tragic Hero

"Man's primary concern is with the rock, with his heart, with tragedy; that is where his hope lies. . . . The forefront of man's mind, and any real future he can contemplate, is occupied with the curiously satisfying taste of the bitter. Sometimes he tires of tasting it, becomes aware of his own contrariness, in effect loses hope. He sees his activity as absurd and invites comedy to make a joke of it. . . . In the reflection of man's choices which drama gives off, tragedy is the positive and comedy is the negative." *(Walter Kerr)*

I

The warrior ethic and the religious and social beliefs fundamental to it establish for each Iliadic man a coherent vision of experience which one can briefly sum up as follows: in a fatalistic universe of constant, irrational, natural cosmic and human strife, where the only certainty man has is the knowledge of his own inevitable death, the final end to his personal existence, the individual has the freedom to choose his response; the finest men, in their freedom, decide to assert their individuality, that is, to define themselves as worthy human beings in battle, risking death in a continuous series of personal encounters in mortal combat. The immediate rewards for the warrior are social esteem and moments of glory in this life and perhaps an enduring fame after death. Each leader organizes his life in the service of this vision; what contributes to it has value, and what does not serve its needs has no place. The warrior code is thus radically pessimistic in the sense not only that the pursuit of personal happiness does not exist as a reasonable option, the choices life offers being inherently unsatisfactory in some important ways, but also that the vision does not provide any acceptable alternative to a chosen life of harsh dangers and either an early death or an insignificant old age. The warrior lives with a cruel destiny which he cannot change, and he constantly strives with all the resources at his command to stand up and declare himself. Only in such a brave reaction does his humanity acquire any value. Such a view of man's lot we can characterize as a tragic vision of experience.

The terms tragic and tragedy in a discussion of a work of literature require some clarification, for these common words in everyday speech often carry a wide range of different meanings. Before we consider the tragic dimension of the *Iliad*, then, it is important to define more precisely the terms central to the discussion. To begin with, we should recognize that the literary critic normally applies the terms tragic and tragedy to two different but related aspects of a literary work: the vision of life which the story or a character in it exemplifies and the structure of the incidents in the narrative, that is, the plot. When we describe a vision of life as tragic, we normally mean that those who believe in it willingly stand up before the realities of fate in the complete awareness of the finality of death, with no paradise beyond, and that they possess a freedom to act upon their own individual values in the face of that unwelcome end. Essential to the notion of the tragic response is the individual hero's sense of his own personal integrity: the highest values in his life depend upon the heroic manifestation in action of his sense of his own rightness, even if such action brings death on more quickly than inaction or compromise. The tragic vision of life thus differs fundamentally from any belief in the progressive amelioration of the given conditions of life, or in the importance of passive submission to destiny, or in the possibility of a finer level of existence after death.

When the term tragedy is applied to the structure of a story, it characteristically means a series of events which ends with the death, usually physical but sometimes emotional, of the main character and the subsequent communal lament over the corpse. The death, however, is not just any demise. For a story to become a tragedy, there must be a necessary connection between the actions of the hero and his death, so that we can see how his destruction results inevitably from a free choice or series of choices he makes in response to a certain event, usually a crisis of some sort. Strictly speaking, therefore, a tragic death can never be merely accidental, although in our everyday language we commonly use the term to describe such unfortunate disasters, since a fortuitous calamity establishes no significant link between the fate of the hero and his actions. Since Aristotle there has been a long and rich debate about the precise meaning of tragedy as an analytic term useful in discussions of literature. Obviously, there is not room here to survey the arguments, but without unjustly oversimplifying a complex issue, we can, I think, accept the basic notion that tragedy is a story in which the hero, by exercising his freedom in response to a particular situation, initiates a series of actions which inevitably brings upon him great suffering and a final death. The last scenes of a dramatic tragedy, the lament over the fallen hero and the carrying out of the corpse, indicate how the structure of the tragic story casts a special emphasis on the significance of a certain individual human being's heroic acceptance of the ultimately fatal demands of his own quest for personal greatness. Tragedy thus has at its very centre a story demonstrating the human willingness to face up to the most terrifying elements of life and to accept the consequences without compromise.[1]

To appreciate this vision of life more fully we can compare it to gentler possibilities in which man turns away from the extreme facts of his own condition and embraces a more acceptable alternative, one that removes from him the sternest demands of his own individuality and finds a significant meaning for life in a retreat or accommodation of some sort. On the basis of this very general distinction, we can usefully contrast the tragic vision of life with its traditional alternative, the comic vision, the crucial difference between the two being their attitudes to the ultimate realities of a fatal condition. The tragic, no matter what the cost, faces up to and accepts extremity; the comic, by contrast, turns away from such an encounter and seeks a compromise.[2] This comparison invites us to recognize in our two oldest and most popular forms of narrative the two most important demands we make upon ourselves: individual integrity in the face of fatal odds and survival within the human community at some cost to our individuality. In this distinction we can see also the point Walter Kerr makes when he talks about how there is always in great tragedy, for all the horrible pain, suffering, and death, something of a joyful triumph and in comedy, for all the communal celebration and fun, something of a defeat. Tragedy forces us to recognize the ways in which the human spirit has the strength and energy to rise above the common lot, to risk everything in the search beyond customary limits for ultimate answers on its own terms; comedy, by contrast, requires a turning away from such a demanding quest and a settling for the less ambitious human pleasures that are possible in an imperfect, evil, but acceptable world of compromise and retreat (Kerr 19). Perhaps, too, in that sense of the comic as a defeat of some kind, we see the origin of the desperate sadness that often lurks beneath the surface of our greatest clowns. Their

---

1 This very brief summary necessarily avoids many controversial questions: for example, the possibilities of traditional Christian tragedy or modern tragedy. I offer it here as an introduction to a concept which a study of the tragic qualities in the Iliad will develop further.
2 In this discussion of tragedy and comedy I am much indebted to the books of Murray Krieger and Walter Kerr.

laughter emerges from some inner acknowledgement that it is the only alternative to a self-destructive effort to rise above the inadequacies of man's lot.

With the above very general comments in mind, we can see that the warrior society in the *Iliad* sustains itself with a tragic vision, but one on which the group has placed important controls. The warrior takes up an aggressively individualistic stance before his irrational destiny and sets at the centre of his system of values the heroic assertion of his own integrity, without the assistance of a faith in reasonable morality or a posthumous region of rewards and punishments. However, as we have already seen, the typical member of this society, like Diomedes or Sarpedon, recognizes certain limits to his engagement with extremity. The code requires him constantly to face the deadly strife honorably, but it also permits him under particular circumstance temporarily to withdraw. The religious metaphor by which he comprehends the world places some restraints on the normal individual's push to the mortal edge of human possibilities. One can decline to engage the gods in combat. Moreover, in his confrontations with the universal powers of fate, the warrior does not have to depend upon his own willed system of meaning; the group around him provides a challenging but also reassuring sense of what he must do from moment to moment. The traditions of his family, his past experience, and his position in the social hierarchy protect the Iliadic leader from the most painful consequences of a fully liberated push for individual glory. Even when he succumbs in his final battle, the group of comrades surrounds him to reassure the dying hero of the rightness of his conduct. Diomedes, for example, understands clearly the limits of his responsibilities as a heroic warrior; he will fight only up to a certain point, but he will not continue once the odds become obviously impossible. Having pursued his *aristeia* up to the wounding of Aphrodite and Ares, he recognizes that he has reached a limit beyond which he cannot go without bringing on certain self-destruction. He thus will not on this occasion follow his heroic spirit, his search for status, glory, and fame, inexorably to its fatal conclusion, for he remains an orthodox and uncritical servant of his society's creed, which requires a controlled heroism, not a full-scale individualistic attack against fate. Similarly, Sarpedon's final battle and dying speech (16.492) confirm his adherence to the same group fighting ethic. He lives and dies a brave warrior, always among his comrades, earning the distinction which his society confers upon him, but he never, and especially not in dying, moves outside the group, physically or spiritually, so that he does not realize his potential for full tragic experience in isolation from the conventional consolations of his society (Mueller, "Knowledge and Delusion" 108).

Hence, while Diomedes and Sarpedon are important warrior leaders and military heroes, they do not have the pre-eminent stature of tragic heroes. However much they assert their individuality and repeatedly risk death in the process, they still remain servants of the faith which unites all the warriors, and to that extent their lives do not illustrate the tragic consequences of a full emancipation of the individual from all ethical restraint, that characteristic which informs the ultimate quest of the tragic hero of the poem, Akhilleus. There is, after all, an important difference between the hero who suffers and dies among friends and fellow-believers in the service of a popular cause for which he is an unquestioning and faithful apologist and the hero who suffers and dies alone in a personal search for an answer which he has chosen to demand from fate and which he must have on his own terms. This distinction has occasionally provided some of those who have sought to develop theories of tragedy a good deal of difficulty (Friedrich Schiller, for example), especially when they want to reconcile with existing moral principles the radically emotional, irrational stance of the individual isolated from any conventional system of belief. We can recognize the significance of the distinction in our sense that in some important manner Hektor and Akhilleus are qualitatively different from everyone else in the poem and that our response to them has something to do with the way in which the two men move beyond the normal experience of the individual in the larger group into a strange and frightening realm of individual isolation before their fatal destiny.

Still, for all the differences between the normal leaders and the two great heroes of the epic, each warrior manifests in his vision of life a tragic potential, a paradoxical interplay between a given fate and his freedom to assert his own value. All events in the poem play themselves out against the well-known fate of these fighting men. The narrative in the *Iliad* always unfolds with the reader's full awareness of the larger plot, the destructive outcome of the war. Tragedy relies heavily upon the way in which very familiar stories from the past ensure that the reader possesses from the outset the essential knowledge of how the plot will conclude; in that sense, there is little narrative suspense in a tragedy. Unless the storyteller has, like Euripides or Brecht, a desire to attack with a satiric surprise conclusion the tragic vision itself, the familiar tale requires the familiar ending. In place of narrative originality, the tragic story creates a pervasive and strong irony: every individual decision, hope, and action we measure against our knowledge of the final outcome. And the prophetic speeches of the heroes and the gods (for example, Zeus' foretelling the deaths of Patroklos, Sarpedon, and Hektor and the fall of Troy in 15.49 or Hektor's sense of the final result of the war in 6.441) remind us again and again of the ironic contrast between human hopes and human fate and generate a continuing emotional tension throughout the poem.

However, if we sense, in the inexorable movement towards a known ending, the actions of an omnipotent fate, that does not mean that the human actions are predestined or that the characters have no freedom. What commands our fullest imaginative assent is the heroic willingness of these warriors to defend their integrity, to follow the logic of the choices they have made right up until death. To introduce into a discussion of the *Iliad* the notion that all the significant actions of the heroes, including their decision to fight, arise from forces outside human control, and thus to suggest that they have no freedom to choose and are compelled to act the way they do, removes from them the human quality of vital individuality, their most impressive characteristic. The tragic stance of the Iliadic warrior may be difficult fully to comprehend, but labels which deprive them of their freedom and their human integrity prevent the reader from recognizing the rich humanness of this demanding code.[3] Even if the normal warrior-leaders always stop short of personally taking their relationship with the irrational universe to an individually determined limit and, by remaining within the shared code which defines their value and their immediate duties, restrict their quest for a personal encounter with extremity, we repeatedly see them freely affirming the rightness of their decision to act in a certain manner and recommitting themselves to the fight. In fact, the only characters who are truly free in the *Iliad* are those who have accepted the warrior code, who have chosen, that is, to define their integrity day by day in a public demonstration of courage and loyalty under conditions of the utmost danger. We still admire that quality in human beings, especially in those who exemplify it to the highest degree. Thus, we respond with imaginative sympathy and even awe to heroically tragic characters whom in all other respects we might despise (Macbeth, for example). Whether we find such people agreeable social personalities is irrelevant. By their nature, tragic characters are often not very likeable; those who in a tremendous and frequently violent burst of self-assertion contradict our civilized norms inevitably, to a greater or lesser extent, offend our social sensibilities. For all our imaginative wonder at their greatness, who would want Akhilleus, Aias, Lear, or even Oedipus as a next-door neighbor?

---

3 Note, for example, the following comment from Jaynes: "The Trojan war was directed by hallucinations. And the soldiers who were so directed were not at all like us. They were noble automatons who knew not what they did" (75).

II

Among the Iliadic leaders Hektor obviously stands out as a special case. That he possesses an importance greater than that of any other warrior apart from Akhilleus no reader will deny. But the precise significance of his special greatness occasions some dispute. Hektor is the unquestioned leader of the Trojans, and throughout most of the poem he acts in a way quite typical of a pre-eminent warrior. Unlike Agamemnon, he displays no uncharacteristic hesitation or uncertainly about what his responsibilities demand, except immediately before his final encounter. His authority as the foremost fighting man in Troy and his qualities as a leader no one ever doubts, at least not until Poulydamas' suggestion of alternative tactics (18.254). Before Akhilleus' return to the war, Hektor is one of the most successful followers and clearest exponents of the warrior faith. As we have seen, even when his behaviour brings out very clearly some of the more obvious ironies of that code, as in the scene with Andromakhe and Astyanax, for example, he remains an uncritical servant of his culture's vision of life. His attitude to the gods and their treatment of him reveal no significant differences between Hektor and the other warriors, except in degree. His conduct on the battlefield, including his many triumphs and his setbacks, his being wounded, and his recovering with the help of Apollo, presents nothing really new in the poem. Throughout most of the *Iliad* Hektor conducts himself in accordance with the normal demands of the group; he is just more successful than most.

But the scene of Hektor's death introduces something very different; it gives him a unique significance in the epic. For in the fatal encounter with Akhilleus in Book Twenty-two, Homer introduces some important departures from normality. Before his final battle, Hektor, for the very first time, becomes totally isolated, physically displaced from his comrades. He has enjoyed dazzling success and a cruel reversal in leading the Trojans against the Akhaian ships. Now he stands alone outside the walls of the city; his parents have made their most eloquent pleas for his return. Hektor must decide whether to face Akhilleus or to retreat within the walls, declining battle. His moment of supreme crisis has come. Hektor's first reaction to this untypical situation is, as we have seen earlier, to reaffirm the code which has served him so well in the past. He weighs the options he has. If he returns inside the walls, people will laugh at him, and he will suffer the worst criticism he can imagine, public shame for his battlefield conduct (22.99). By comparison with that certain result, he prefers his chances against Akhilleus. But then, in his

97

physical isolation, Hektor suddenly changes his mind and starts examining ways to avoid the conflict. He briefly considers betraying everything he has lived for, by throwing himself on the mercy of Akhilleus, offering enormous gifts, half the wealth of the city and Helen as well. Hektor apparently realizes how abnormal such an action would be, for he acknowledges that he would have to take an oath to divide Troy's wealth without deceit, the first suggestion of the potential for dishonest conduct in a noble warrior. That possibility he then rejects as impractical and dishonorable. Akhilleus may spurn his offer and kill him anyway, thus redoubling his shame. And so he returns once more to the simple clarity of the warrior code: "Better we duel, now at once, and see to whom the Olympian awards the glory" (22.129). Hektor's hesitation here--his summoning up, even momentarily, dishonorable options--indicates that his faith has started to disintegrate; it has become uncharacteristically difficult for him to meet the present situation with the customary heroic response.[4]

Hektor's behaviour at the first appearance of Akhilleus suggests, then, that the strain of adhering to the community ethic has become so strong that Hektor, in his physical isolation, has great trouble maintaining it. He does not want to act in the way which his vision of life tells him he must; nothing in the code will justify the options he would prefer to attempt. And so Hektor does the unthinkable: he runs away. Hektor's instinctive flight indicates that he has momentarily lost the will to continue the heroic role, that the warrior's faith no longer answers his most urgent emotional demands, to evade the wrath of Akhilleus, and so he breaks down. In other words, because he is at a total loss, left with nothing to guide him but a sudden onrush of fear, he panics and surrenders himself to the most human of impulses, a desperate attempt to escape certain death. Instantly, the significance of his life collapses, and his existence turns into a nightmare.

> *As in a dream a man chasing another*
> *cannot catch him, nor can he in flight*
> *escape from his pursuer, so Akhilleus*
> *could not by his swiftness overtake him,*
> *nor could Hektor pull away. (22.199)*

4 Those who seek to understand Hektor by paying close attention to his psychology, not always the most reliable way of understanding the characters in the Iliad, may see an important connection between his conscious hesitation here and the unconscious ironies evoked in his conversation with Andromakhe in Book Six. Redfield offers the illuminating suggestion that Hektor's terror at the gleaming armour of the approaching Akhilleus is a deliberate reminder of Astyanax's terror at the sight of his father's military appearance earlier (158). Hektor's momentary doubt immediately before his duel with Telamonian Aias may be significant in this regard (7.216).

The extended description of Hektor's running away in repetitive circles around Troy illustrates the absurdity of life from which the heroic assertion of individual meaning has disappeared. The heroic code does not permit Hektor to enter Troy, and his personal feelings do not permit him to stand and fight. The once proud warrior has consequently become totally disoriented, like a terrified rabbit, because the faith that has sustained him is inadequate, and he does not know what to do, or rather, he cannot endure doing what he knows he must. In that absence of a faith in heroic self-assertion, how else can a man cope with the terrible fear of death but run until the destroyer catches him? But Hektor has nowhere to run to. Caught in an acute dilemma from which there is no way out, he instinctively changes his heroic path, up this point in his life always a direct linear course to and from battle, into an absurd, never-ending circular chase in no-man's-land. The passage offers no suggestion that Hektor is aware why he is behaving in this way; he does not even consciously decide to run. Once his creed starts to fail him, his heroic control disintegrates, and he loses command of his physical movements.

Significantly, Hektor regains his heroic composure as soon as he meets a comrade. With Deiphobos apparently at his side, Hektor instantly rediscovers the warrior code which had failed him when he was alone, and he can now move to face Akhilleus in the conventional manner. Having accepted the strong likelihood of his death, he seeks to bargain with Akhilleus to make sure that he receives the traditional funeral honours. The latter's fierce, uncompromising refusal indicates that he is following a very different vision from Hektor's customary faith. This Hektor does not see; back in the only system of belief he has ever experienced, he seeks to hang onto the certainties it offers. Even when he recognizes Athena's trick and faces the sure knowledge of his own imminent death, Hektor indicates that he will die as he has lived, firmly inside the community ethic.

> "This is the end. The gods are calling deathward.
> I had thought
> a good soldier, Dêíphobos, was with me.
> He is inside the walls. Athêna tricked me.
> Death is near, and black, not at a distance,
> not to be evaded. Long ago
> this hour must have been to Zeus's liking
> and to the liking of his archer son.
> They have been well disposed before, but now
> the appointed time's upon me. Still, I would not
> die without delivering a stroke,
> or die ingloriously, but in some action
> memorable to men in days to come." (22.297)

The speech expresses the calm, heroic resolution and the great courage of a man determined to live up to the highest standards of his way of life. Hektor's reaffirmation of his society's creed means that he dies a loyal member of the group. His panic isolates him for a time, but before his death he has returned to what he has always been. In other words, at his moment of greatest personal crisis, Hektor is unable to push beyond the normal code of conduct; he panics, recovers himself, and then, like so many other warriors, at his death he takes refuge in it. This speech does not, then, reveal an extraordinary insight into human life, a more intense and deeper vision than the knowledge granted to the normal warrior-leader, an insight earned through immense personal suffering. It rather demonstrates Hektor's inability to rise to the full tragic awareness of his human condition. In a sense, by recalling himself to the traditional notion of his duty and invoking the conventional language of his warrior code, Hektor is protecting himself. He has not re-embraced his customary faith because he has freely chosen to do so, in the full light of its consequences, returning to the orthodox fold with the fresh and vital awareness of a temporary apostate. He is grabbing hold of it, as if it were the only guard against a total loss of meaning in his final moments. His dying request to Akhilleus for proper treatment of his corpse is thus an apparently vain last invocation of the customary rituals, a final plea for the traditional honours which confer meaning onto a battlefield death. And when Akhilleus' refusal to honour Hektor's dying words reveals again just how far the victor has moved from normal conduct, how impervious he is to the group expectations, Hektor can only make the desperately weak dying reply that the gods may punish Akhilleus if he does not behave properly.

Hektor's last combat thus presents a cruelly ironic portrait of a victim of the heroic code rather than an uplifting tragic experience. Hektor's death is not, by his own standards, absurd, as it might have been if Akhilleus had speared him in the back while he was running away. The assertion of his heroic dignity, however, is undercut by our sense that in his desperation he is using tradition as an inadequate illusion. Hektor must know before he dies that his life will count for something, and the only system of values he can reach for is the traditional one which has just failed him. True, Hektor has regained his courageous composure, but the experience of collapse has not brought him to a significantly new awareness of his condition. Hence, Hektor's death scene does not support the contention that he dies in full tragic glory, that he somehow gains an insight into the absolute verities of human existence, that before his death "he sees the whole truth; in the face of it, the flaw which false hope had made in his courage is cured, and he meets Achilles like an equal" (Whitman 212), or that "At this moment, and only at this moment, Hektor is equal to Achilles, and superior to all Iliadic characters, in the depth and intensity of his consciousness of life as limited and valorized by the fact of death" (Mueller, *Iliad*, 64), or that at this moment he is "endowed with a brief moment of clairvoyance" (Michalopoulos 95). To equate Hektor and Akhilleus here, or to compare Hektor with Oedipus, is to invest Hektor's death speeches with a significance they will not support.[5] For there is no sense that Akhilleus and Hektor meet here as equals. Quite the contrary. Hektor remains an admirable human warrior-leader, but Akhilleus we know is on a different plane altogether. The spiritual difference between the two is as marked as the difference between the normal armour of Akhilleus which Hektor is wearing and the divinely created armour of his opponent.

Akhilleus' immense physical, emotional, and spiritual superiority over Hektor in this encounter is perhaps one reason why many readers find Hektor a far more sympathetic figure than Akhilleus. The preference rests not only on our natural liking for the leader of the most famous underdogs in our best-known war, who will soon lose everything to the cruel victors, or on our natural admiration for the chief of those fighting in defense of their homes and families, or even on the way in which our Christian tradition can more easily ascribe to Hektor orthodox moral virtues. We also like Hektor because we can readily understand what has happened to him. In comparison with Akhilleus' ruthless confidence, brutal success, and terrifying spiritual isolation, Hektor's momentary loss of faith and the emotional uncertainties of his final battle strike us as particularly human, actions we ourselves might well demonstrate in the fatal ironies of the killing zone.

III

As well as presenting the tragic sense of the warrior life, the *Iliad* also tells the story of Akhilleus, the first great tragic hero in our culture.

---

5 See, for example, Mueller's linking Oedipus and Hektor in "Knowledge and Delusion" (115). If one wants to make comparisons, Hektor is surely far closer to Hotspur or, perhaps, to Othello. T. S. Eliot's comment on Othello, in my view, comes close to describing Hektor's final moments: "Humility is the most difficult of all virtues to achieve; nothing dies harder than the desire to think well of oneself. Othello succeeds in turning himself into a pathetic figure, by adopting an aesthetic rather than a moral attitude, dramatizing himself against the environment. He takes in the spectator, but the human motive is primarily to take in himself" (130).

He is, beyond all doubt, the central character in the poem, as the opening invocation announces, because in his experience of the war he develops a personal tragic sense of human life and explores the extreme consequences of that vision with an integrity and an intensity that no one else in the poem even understands, let alone imitates.[6] In examining the story of Akhilleus throughout the *Iliad*, the reader necessarily has to confront the mysterious and extraordinary human greatness of the uncompromising heroic search for ultimate meaning in an irrational and dangerous world. Whatever we may feel about Akhilleus as a character, and many of the actions he undertakes are shockingly cruel and even, at times, absurd, Homer's story of the great hero forces us to recognize in his life the unique magnificence of the tragic response in a particularly great individual.

It is possible to distinguish a number of separate stages through which Akhilleus passes on the route to his final calm anticipation of his own death. First, the poem depicts him as a famous but recognizably normal heroic warrior. After the quarrel, he enters a period of unusual inactivity, in which for several books he disappears from the poem, and when he does reappear it is evident that some important changes have taken place. In his remarkable reaction to the death of Patroklos, Akhilleus reveals yet another development, and this change leads directly to his decision to re-enter the war and to his subsequent *aristeia*. Finally, after the killing of Hektor, in the most extraordinary scene in the poem, a transformed Akhilleus meets Priam to arrange the surrender of Hektor's corpse. By the end of the narrative, the normal warrior of the opening has become so changed that he is quite unlike any of his former comrades: he exists in the glorious and complex isolation of one who has experienced, through intense emotional dislocation and suffering, a different order of reality and who can therefore no longer return with unquestioning faith to the traditional ethic of the group from which he departed only a few days before.

At the very start of the poem, Akhilleus appears indistinguishable from the other warrior-leaders, except for his strength, speed, and past success, and later on the various references to his earlier exploits (for example, Andromakhe's tale of the destruction of her family in 6.407) indicate that up to this point his career has followed the traditional path. In Book One other leaders acknowledge Akhilleus' military prowess, a gift from the gods, but they accord him no unique honour in the peer group other than that, and Nestor, the voice of traditional authority,

---

6 One of the great merits of Cedric Whitman's study of the Iliad in Homer and the Heroic Tradition, a study to which I owe a great deal, is the central emphasis the author gives to the career of Akhilleus.

makes clear the relationship between Agamemnon's and Akhilleus' relative social positions. Akhilleus' reaction to the confiscation of Briseis is what we would expect from any other warrior-chief: great rage over the loss of status which the public removal of girl represents. And his unusual decision to withdraw his and his men's services from the battle represents a logical, if somewhat extreme, response to Agamemnon's foolishness. The anger he unleashes on the Akhaians, prophesying disaster for the army, and his own vow not to help arise out of his feelings that the social code has let him down--a very passionate outburst, to be sure, but not yet a conscious decision to abandon his faith in his society. His action registers as the naturally emotional behaviour of a proud leader whose public reputation has been severely injured; it does not declare an overt denial of everything that has made Akhilleus great. In fact, by hoping that his withdrawal will shame Agamemnon in front of everyone else, Akhilleus is obviously relying upon the traditional code to effect his desires. The language of his oath, however, contains ironic suggestions that Akhilleus does not recognize the full significance of what this moment will bring.

> "But here is what I say: my oath upon it
> by this great staff: look: leaf or shoot
> it cannot sprout again, once lopped away
> from the log it left behind in the timbered hills;
> it cannot flower, peeled of bark and leaves;
> instead, Akhaian officers in council
> take it in hand by turns, when they observe
> by the will of Zeus due order in debate:
> let this be what I swear by then: I swear
> a day will come when every Akhaian soldier
> will groan to have Akhilleus back. That day
> you shall no more prevail on me than this
> dry wood shall flourish. . . ."   (1.233)

His words here offer a richly ironic insight into the origin and the future course of Akhilleus' tragedy. He takes his oath on the most important emblem of traditional respect among his peers, the object symbolizing "by the will of Zeus due order in debate." In accordance with the freedom that tradition grants to each warrior, Akhilleus declares his choice and confirms it by reminding the assembly of the ancient authority for his actions. Then he hurls the staff to the ground. Obviously, in his anger, he means to indicate to his peers as dramatically as possible his most passionate feelings about Agamemnon's insult. But by throwing away the symbol of their common religious and political ethic, Akhilleus unwittingly reveals the deeper consequences of his action: he is rejecting the group and therefore the communal warrior faith which gives him the only system of meaning in the world he understands and which has made him what he is. After all, Agamemnon's insult only makes sense within the context of the orthodox warrior culture, and Akhilleus' extreme reaction to the king's arrogance illustrates just how thoroughly he is a product of the group creed. His immediate motive may be passionate anger and a desire to teach the Akhaians just how important he is, but the dramatic gesture indicates to the reader the beginning of an emotional and a spiritual displacement. Out of an understandable reaction to the confiscation of the girl, Akhilleus has initiated, without yet fully realizing the fact, a process that will alienate him from the group, whose leader, he feels, has failed to honour him sufficiently.

The poetic imagery of Akhilleus' oath, too, conveys the hidden complexity of the moment. The wooden staff will never flourish again, for it has been cut away from its nourishment, its tree and its environment, and is now dead. Akhilleus' emphasis upon that image in the very course of cutting himself away from the organism which has nourished him raises the question: How is he to flourish now that he denies the only system of values he has ever known? And the implied comparison with the staff indicates an answer: dry, dead wood flourishes again, if at all, only in fire, for only in the glorious blaze which destroys what it feeds on can the lopped-off limb regain vital heat and become, in a process of self-destruction, a beautiful living thing. Here again, Akhilleus is announcing no carefully thought-out plan; his oath and his rejection of the staff are spontaneous responses to his deepest feelings, in his view quite appropriate to the insult he has received. But the dramatic irony latent in the imagery--the gap between our complete understanding of what the moment represents and Akhilleus' only very partial grasp of its significance--alerts us to the full implications not only of the action but also of Akhilleus' ignorance. This dramatic irony receives further emphasis a few lines later when Akhilleus asks his mother, Thetis, to secure Zeus's favour in giving help to the Trojans, so that events will shame Agamemnon. Thetis responds with a lament for the untimely death of her son. At this moment, Akhilleus' death is the furthest thing from his mind--he wants revenge; but Thetis and the reader see the more profound significance of the action which initiates Akhilleus' tragic story.

In that dramatic irony, we discover Akhilleus' *hamartia*, the tragic ignorance of the consequences of his passionate actions. This famous Aristotelian term is often rendered into English with the phrase "tragic flaw," an expression that sometimes causes difficulties. For it can encourage those who wish to moralize the tragic experience, who wish, that is, to subsume its complex insights under a rational system which enables them to draw a specific and reasonable moral from the story, to understand by the word "flaw" some moral imperfection, some corrigible human character trait which deserves punishment. Critics who interpret *hamartia* in this way often display an unfortunate tendency to reduce the tragic narrative at all costs into a simple morality piece illustrating the hero's chastisement for sin or immaturity (for example, Oedipus' pride, Macbeth's ambition, Lear's vanity, Klytaimnestra's lust, and so on). It is important to recognize, however, that Akhilleus' *hamartia*, like that of other great tragic heroes, arises from the best part of his human nature, that the anger he exhibits here springs from the same qualities that have made him a mighty warrior. Far from being a sinner, Akhilleus is a magnificently successful human leader, and those characteristics which have made him worthy in the past prompt his actions at the initial moment of crisis. If he were less impressively and vitally human, he would not display the "flaw," but then he would not be the great man he is. The irony of his unwitting displacement from the group demonstrates that his *hamartia*, like that of Oedipus, arises from his ignorance, the very human ignorance about the fatal consequences of a decision taken with the most understandable motives. If we call this a "flaw," we must also acknowledge that it is not a particular moral fault so much as an inescapable element in the human condition, and that only those great souls who have the courage to act decisively as their feelings and imaginations dictate will reveal it.

Furthermore, it is worth stressing that Akhilleus' anger, the outburst which launches his tragedy, comes from an understandable reaction. The anger is very strong, but it originates in the natural feelings of a proud, successful warrior-prince, who up to this point has always conducted himself in accordance with the ethical demands of his society. The anger is not abnormal; nor is Akhilleus, as some critics have insisted, at the start of the poem already in important respects displaced from his fellow Akhaians.[7] By suggesting that Akhilleus is somehow a uniquely different individual even before his physical isolation, such critical claims immediately lessen the human significance of the tragic story of the hero of the *Iliad*, because they inevitably imply that Akhilleus is in some fundamental way odd and therefore quite unlike us. What makes Akhilleus extraordinary, however, is not his initial character or the emotional outburst in the quarrel with Agamemnon, a reaction which the reader can readily comprehend, but rather his persistent refusals to rejoin the group later in the poem, once the consequences of his action, and particularly of his displacement from the activity which has made him what he is, begin to take effect. Nor is there much evidence that all his violent ac-

---

7 Paolo Vivante suggests that Akhilleus' anger is "a divine, not a human emotion" (54), and Schein claims that from the outset of the poem Akhilleus is "radically different from [the other Akhaians]" (91).

cusations against Agamemnon are wholly justified. For Akhilleus has obviously not been treated habitually in an unfair manner; he has done very well in the fighting, and if the commander-in-chief gets more of the spoils, as the warrior code insists, that does not mean that Akhilleus has had to settle for "some trifle." In his anger, Akhilleus is accusing Agamemnon somewhat unfairly, giving vent to overwhelming feelings with reasons that do not fully match the anger which motivates him.

Akhilleus' willed displacement from his peers initiates the chain of events that transforms him from a recognizably normal human being, a great man, into a lonely explorer of the uncharted emotional regions of experience. Before his angry decision, Akhilleus has a recognized place in society and, like everyone else, derives his sense of himself from the conventional beliefs of his peers. Moments later, without his fully realizing what is happening, his transformation begins:

> *Meanwhile unstirring and with smoldering heart,*
> *the godlike athlete, son of Pêleus, Prince*
> *Akhilleus waited by his racing ships.*
> *He would not enter the assembly*
> *of emulous men, nor ever go to war,*
> *but felt his valor staling in his breast*
> *with idleness, and missed the cries of battle. (1.488)*

And soon enough, in this wholly unexpected situation, the normal rules of conduct start to loosen, customary relationships, lines of authority, systems of belief fall away, and before very long he finds himself increasingly on a course where he must travel alone, according to his own rules. The intriguing question, the mystery at the very heart of the tragedy in the *Iliad*, is this: Why does Akhilleus behave in this way? Why does he not choose some less intransigent course, or, more important, having chosen to reject the group, why does he not later relent and rejoin his fellows, especially when his opponent is willing to apologize and repay him many times over for the original insult? There is no simple response to such questions. The first step in the process, the willed movement away from the group, and the decision then to accept the consequences of that isolation without compromise have their origins in the deepest feelings some human beings have about their own personal value. Of course, Akhilleus does not deliberately set out on a self-destructive course, any more than Oedipus, Macbeth, Lear, or other similarly tragic figure does, fully conscious of the conclusion of his choice. On the contrary, Akhilleus, like the other tragic heroes, hopes for nothing but a successful outcome to his plans, and his story, like theirs, is full of the most painfully ironic reversals, which reveal to the reader and finally to the hero himself the full cost of his uncompromising stance before his fate.

Witnessing the moment at which the tragic character, for understandable reasons, launches the course of action which will transform him from a social being into a heroically free, suffering individual is an essential part of any tragedy, for only in relation to what the hero is to begin with, a recognizably ethical man, responsive to the orthodoxy of his social group, can we fully grasp the significance for us of what he becomes, a man who answers to no one but himself. The power of the tragic story lies in the step-by-step metamorphosis with which we can, as fellow human beings, imaginatively sympathize. When a tragedy denies us this moment of initial transformation, when the hero is an outsider alienated from his society at our very first acquaintance with him, we have no way of comprehending exactly why he acts the way he does. Our eternally inconclusive arguments about Hamlet, for example, arise out of our ignorance: we never see him in a recognizably normal state, for by the opening of the play whatever has led to his displacement has already occurred. We hear a great deal about how noble he was before the changes in his disposition, but we never see him in that state, nor does the play show us precisely those actions which have left him isolated and bitter. We can and do produce all sorts of speculative interpretations, but a final consensus eludes us, because we do not have sufficient information. In the *Iliad*, by contrast, the opening book allows us to see and to understand clearly the crucial moment at which Akhilleus, for conventional reasons, rejects convention.

Once Akhilleus removes himself from the group, he disappears from the story for several books, reappearing in Book Nine, when the Akhaians send Odysseus, Phoinix, and Telamonian Aias to persuade him to relent. By this time in the poem we have become thoroughly familiar with the behaviour of the typical warrior-leader in this society, for in the intervening books the battlefield actions of Diomedes, Aias, Menelaos, Odysseus, and Hektor, among others, define for us how normal men, especially the best of them, meet experience and deal with each other. Particularly important in this portrayal of the warrior's life, as we have seen earlier, are the restraints placed upon the individual's desires to transcend or to evade the common code. Consequently, by the time we meet Akhilleus once more we have been well prepared to evaluate just how far he has moved from the group of which he was a fully-fledged, willing, and unquestioning member at the opening of Book One. The Akhaian ambassadors to Akhilleus base their appeal to him, just as Agamemnon does, on their understanding of normal men, assuming that Akhilleus is the same man he has always been. Obviously, according to their vision of human conduct, Akhilleus should relent. His continuing refusal indicates that, however he might have felt at the time of the original quarrel, when such persuasion might have worked to change his mind, the inexorable emotional logic of his choice has been at work in the interval he has been away from the fighting.

Odysseus first provides the details of Agamemnon's apology and compensation for the insult (9.225). Whatever we may think of the sometimes erratic behaviour of the commander-in-chief, his compensation is extraordinarily munificent, marks of the very highest status. It would be difficult to imagine what else Agamemnon could have added to the rich offer of gold, horses, towns, spoils, daughters, and dowry. To provide an added incentive Odysseus stresses the pain Akhilleus will have to endure if he stands idly by while the Argives die. Akhilleus rejects the offer at once, and the unequivocal certainty of his reasons indicates that away from the field he has developed an even more passionate sense of the absolute rightness of his personal feelings.

> *"No need to sit with me like mourning doves*
> *making your gentle noise by turns. I hate*
> *as I hate Hell's own gate that man who hides*
> *one thought within him while he speaks another.*
> *What I shall say is what I see and think.*
> *Give in to Agamémnon? I think not,*
> *neither to him nor to the rest. I had*
> *small thanks for fighting, fighting without truce*
> *against hard enemies here. The portion's equal*
> *whether a man hangs back or fights his best;*
> *the same respect, or lack of it, is given*
> *brave man and coward."*   (9.311)

We should not confuse Akhilleus' emotional desires here with the particular reasons he gives. We know, for example, that he has received ample rewards in the fighting, and Agamemnon's offer would be more than sufficient to persuade any normal man, if his sole concern was tangible manifestations of his fighting prowess and public status. After all, the extravagance of the compensation indicates just how highly the king values Akhilleus. Moreover, Akhilleus' complaint about everyone getting equal portions is obviously incorrect in the context of the offer we have just listened to; furthermore, his speech contains a clear indication of just how much he has gained materially from the war ("now I take home gold and ruddy bronze, and women belted luxuriously, and hoary iron, all that came to me here"). The inadequacy of the reason, like the absolute refusal to admit any sort of compromise into his dealings with other men, shows that Akhilleus' refusal here rests on something else, on his personal determination to stand apart. Akhilleus may believe what he states, but the logic of his refusal does not bear close scrutiny, especially in the extreme language he uses in lines like the following:

> *"he robbed me blind,*
> *broke faith with me: he gets no second chance*
> *to play me for a fool. Once is enough." (9.375)*

> *"Not if his gifts outnumbered the sea sands*
> *or all the dust grains in the world could Agamémnon*
> *ever appease me--not till he pays me back*
> *full measure, pain for pain, dishonor for dishonor." (9.385)*

His attitude has become, like Lear's, thoroughly disproportionate to the original insult. Consequently, even if Akhilleus apparently defines the injuries done to him in terms of the warrior code, he is, in fact, now developing a much more passionately uncompromising personal sense of righteousness and is rapidly leaving conventional behaviour far behind him. Putting the matter another way, we can say that Akhilleus's new feelings about himself have outgrown his ability to explain them; he reaches for the conventional vocabulary of his past to account for his present attitudes, but his appeal to the code cannot properly describe the personal spiritual struggle his original decision has initiated. Already he is traveling through emotions unknown to him earlier or to his peers.

Confirmation of the significant changes taking place in Akhilleus' view of himself comes in the references to a different vision of life.

> *"Why must Argives*
> *fight the Trojans? Why did he raise an army*
> *and lead it here? For Helen, was it not?*
> *Are the Atreidai of all mortal men*
> *the only ones who love their wives? I think not.*
> *Every sane decent fellow loves his own*
> *and cares for her, as in my heart I loved*
> *Brisêis, though I won her by the spear." (9.337)*

> *"And if the great Earthshaker gives a breeze,*
> *the third day out I'll make it home to Phthía.*
> *Rich possessions are there I left behind*
> *when I was mad enough to come here...." (9.362)*

> *"There in my manhood I have longed, indeed,*
> *to marry someone of congenial mind*
> *and take my ease, enjoying the great estate*
> *my father had acquired.*
>
> *Now I think*
> *no riches can compare with being alive,*
> *not even those they say this well-built Ilion*
> *stored up in peace before the Akhaians came." (9.398)*

No wonder when Akhilleus finishes "all were silent, awed" (9.430), for the attitude in these comments is heretical, an overt renunciation of everything these men (including Akhilleus, a particularly successful member of the warrior group) and their ancestors have believed for as long as they can remember. To offer love as a replacement for status, home possessions for booty, peaceful leisure for heroic effort, and life for fame--all this astonishes his listeners. Akhilleus' separation from his peers, his inactivity, and his powerful emotional reaction to that unusual condition have led him to sense, however intermittently, alternatives to the warrior's orthodoxy. It is important to note here that these comments do not define a new faith on Akhilleus' part, for in the passionate and often illogical appeals both to the traditional beliefs and to antithetical principles the speech expresses considerable confusion. But the mere fact that Akhilleus can say and think such things shocks his audience; they no longer recognize the man who walked away from the council. And the reader sees clearly enough what has happened: in his rejection of his society, Akhilleus' traditional beliefs are falling away and to sustain his faith in himself he is exploring hitherto unthought of possibilities.

The second spokesman for the embassy, Phoinix, the old family friend and military teacher of Akhilleus, appeals to him in the name of their affection for each other and of ancient precedents for heroic relenting. The speech contains much more personal warmth than do the opening remarks of Odysseus, but the effect on Akhilleus is much the same. In his rejection of Phoinix's view of honour, a much friendlier rejoinder than the one to Odysseus, Akhilleus makes an especially significant remark:

> *"Honored I think I am by Zeus's justice,*
> *justice that will sustain me by the ships*
> *as long as breath is in me and I can stand.*
> *Here is another point: ponder it well:*
> *best not confuse my heart with lamentation*
> *for Agamémnon, whom you must not honor;*
> *you would be hateful to me, dear as you are.*
> *Loyalty should array you at my side*
> *in giving pain to him who gives me pain."* (9.608)

In the intense conviction of his own rightness and to quell any lingering doubts he has about his own conduct, Akhilleus demands a total lack of compromise and a denial of the recognition that loyalty works both ways. So powerful are his feelings about himself that he can equate his own personal emotions with the justice of Zeus, an astonishingly bold, egocentric claim, and insist that anyone who disagrees with him in any way is hateful. At this juncture we might well point out that if loyalty re-

110

quires one to fight on behalf of those who pain one's friends, then what about Akhilleus' obligations to fight Hektor, who is providing much more than pain for the Akhaians. There would be little point in making this argument to Akhilleus, however, since he would be unable to perceive the logic in it, so governed is he now by his own conceptions of what constitutes appropriate conduct.

The final speech of the Akhaian embassy--the shortest and the most effective--comes from Telamonian Aias. He bases his appeal to Akhilleus on the "affections of his friends who made him honored above all others on the beachhead" (9.630). This traditional plea from one fellow warrior to another, and especially Aias' masterful rhetorical tactic of directing most of the speech at Odysseus, as if Akhilleus had disappeared from their company, an action which, by his refusals, Akhilleus has, in a sense, already undertaken, wring from Akhilleus the concession that he may return under certain conditions: once Hektor reaches the ships and burns them, he will reconsider. Some sense of normal human social feeling remains alive in Akhilleus; Aias, the brave fellow-warrior, almost as famous in battle as Akhilleus, makes contact with it by the simplest appeal to friendship among peers who have faced countless mortal dangers together. The gesture Akhilleus makes in response promises nothing definite, but the change in tone and the suggestion of a reconciliation reminds the reader that Akhilleus, for all his peremptory dismissal of Odysseus, has not yet totally isolated himself from his fellows.

The scene of the Argive embassy merits close attention because it shows us that, while the customary battles have been going on, something much more unusual and significant has been taking place by the inactive ship at the end of the Akhaian line. Akhilleus has emancipated himself from the demands of war, but, in so doing, he has, in his freedom from normal restraint, chosen a course of action which brings out hitherto concealed possibilities of individual assertiveness. His actions arise from his own free choice; there is no sense of determinism or predestination about his situation. But the ominous suggestion presents itself that he is heading for a direct confrontation with the elemental, irrational, contradictory powers of natural and cosmic order, carrying with him only the extraordinary force of his own highly charged sense of personal rectitude. The angry pique of the original quarrel with Agamemnon is changing into something much more profound, complex, and dangerous: the spiritual isolation of a man who acknowledges no authority save that of his own passionate will.

When Hektor succeeds in breaching the Akhaian rampart and firing the ships, Akhilleus does indeed reconsider, and that decision leads to his re-entry into the war. To grasp the significance of this change, we need to examine the role of Patroklos, Akhilleus' dearest friend, whose death drives Akhilleus back to battle. At first, Patroklos appears unexceptional, another warrior among many. As a member of Akhilleus' personal retinue, Patroklos listens to him singing, pours wine for the ambassadors from Agamemnon, tends to the fire, prepares a bed for Phoinix, and sleeps with a woman in the same hut as Akhilleus. Later, in Book Eleven he goes to get information about the wounded Akhaians and to treat Eurypylos. Then he returns to Akhilleus and begs permission to help his comrades by going back into the battle. The pattern of these actions gradually develops the sense of Patroklos as an unusually kind man, attentive to the needs of others and sensitive to their distress. Amid the determinedly assertive individual warriors, Patroklos appears something of an exception, moved more by simple human concerns for his friends than by the more selfish demands of the heroic code. Certainly, no other warrior, on either side, makes a plea more squarely based on simple concern for others than does Patroklos at the opening of Book Sixteen. Unlike Agamemnon's worry about his brother's wound or Hektor's about Andromakhe's future, Patroklos' anxiety here is disinterested; he seeks permission to return to battle not to enhance his reputation but to provide badly needed assistance for "our worn-out men." Menelaos' later tribute to Patroklos' "warmth of heart" and his "way of being kind to all in life" (17.671) calls attention to these unique features of Patroklos' personality.

The combination of Patroklos' qualities--his constant attendance upon Akhilleus, his warm concern for others, the strong sense of mutual love between the two men, and the unique duties he has from his father to care for Akhilleus--"to let him hear close reasoning and counsel, even commands" (11.788)--suggests that his relationship with Akhilleus has a particularly important symbolic function. Patroklos gradually emerges as Akhilleus' alter ego, the more sympathetically human side of his stern character. Patroklos' compassionate attachment to his fellow soldiers represents a quality that Akhilleus, in his isolation, has rejected, but the love Akhilleus has for Patroklos keeps alive in his spirit at least some feelings for the warmth of human friendship and loyalty to the community. Whether we see Patroklos and Akhilleus as the two side of the same man or as two quite separate individuals does not really matter; in his obvious care for Patroklos, Akhilleus displays a part of his nature quite different from the heroic individual assertiveness with which he conducts himself before everyone else, and so long as Patroklos remains alive, Akhilleus still has an essential link with the rest of humanity.[8] His

---

8 In this respect, the relationship between Akhilleus and Patroklos has some obvious similarities to that between Lear and his fool, or Hamlet and Horatio, or Coriolanus and his wife.

love for a sympathetic, compassionate friend reminds us that Akhilleus is not devoid of common human feelings, even if he is in the grip of fatal passions which threaten to extinguish those gentler emotions. Hence, we can readily appreciate not only why Akhilleus agrees to Patroklos' tearful request to help the Akhaians but also why he gives him his personal armour. Of course, there is a tactical reason (to pretend to the Trojans that the greatest Akhaian hero has abandoned his inactivity), but the return of Patroklos in the armour of Akhilleus indicates also that an essential part of Akhilleus himself has responded to the dire needs of his old comrades. In this regard, it is worth noting that the entire sequence of events which leads to Patroklos' return to the war and thus to Akhilleus' tragic career is initiated by Akhilleus himself, for his response to the sight of his old comrades in great difficulties prompts him to send Patroklos out to get information about the progress of the battle (11.608). Moreover, if we recognize in the relationship between Akhilleus and Patroklos the last vestige of Akhilleus' most basic emotional links with his fellow men, with what he used to be, then we can much more readily grasp the significance of Akhilleus' enormous grief at Patroklos' death and the extraordinary measures Akhilleus takes to provide proper funeral rites for his friend. Akhilleus is here lamenting and burying himself--or at least that part which makes him a living, loving, human being, an important member of the community--and is thus accepting his permanent isolation from his fellow men.

In granting permission to Patroklos to return to the battle, Akhilleus significantly appears torn between his humane feelings, his desire for a normal life among his peers, and his new wish for tragic isolation. For example, his first instructions suggest that Akhilleus has abandoned his lonely quest for ultimate justice in accordance with his own sense of things.

> "*Now carry out the purpose I confide,*
> *so that you'll win great honor for me, and glory*
> *among Danááns; then they'll send me back*
> *my lovely girl, with bright new gifts as well.*" (16.83)

Akhilleus could have achieved these goals long before, by agreeing to Agamemnon's offer of recompense. Nothing Patroklos does now will win for him honours equal to the quality of the king's earlier gifts. That Akhilleus should suggest such matters at this juncture indicates that part of him is still responding very strongly to the conventional ways of dealing among men. And the restraints he places upon Patroklos (not to attack the city itself but to stop once he has saved the ships) make perfect sense in the normal course of warrior conduct. Akhilleus' prohibitions tell Patroklos that he must not overstep the boundaries of appropriate behaviour. A few lines later, however, Akhilleus reveals again just how powerful the other side of his nature, the uncompromisingly tragic awareness, has become.

> *"Ah, Father Zeus, Athêna, and Apollo!*
> *If not one Trojan of them all*
> *should get away from death, and not one Argive*
> *save ourselves were spared, we two alone*
> *could pull down Troy's old coronet of towers!"* (16.97)

By any normal standard, this wish is quite absurd. It obviously contradicts the very human desire of Patroklos to help his comrades in their most dangerous moments; that is, it flies in the face of the logic that is spurring him to return to the fight. It also denies Akhilleus' express wish a few lines earlier for a return of the girl and more honours from the Akhaians. For if Akhilleus and Patroklos could indeed achieve what these lines imagine, who would be left to confer gifts, status, and value? The source of all these would have disappeared. The emotional demand makes sense, however: Akhilleus wants to push his tragic isolation to the limit, without compromising himself by rejoining the community or bringing any credit to Agamemnon, but he does not want to pay as the price for that his relationship with Patroklos, that is, his sense of his own ability to love and care for his fellow men. He wishes to be rid of all human beings around him, comrades and enemies, for that will vindicate him in his own eyes, and yet he also wishes to retain his full humanity. In the very process of expressing his desires, he exposes their paradoxical impossibility.

At this stage of his story, then, Akhilleus in his freedom has committed himself to having everything that he can imagine life offers. He will be great on his own terms, without retreating from the decisions he has made to ostracize himself from the community and to act according to his own vision of what he should do; at the same time he will retain his full humanity, his sense of the joy in being a great man among other men, loving them and sharing their common human concerns. His quality as a tragic hero comes from the enormity of this contradictory wish and the passion and single-mindedness with which he pursues it, no matter what the cost. He will not admit, as lesser men must, that he cannot have both total individual freedom to act as his emotions dictate and the significant personal relationships which confer social value upon him and which arise out of the ties that bind. Akhilleus here is like Oedipus, who in his freedom has chosen to solve the mystery of Laius' murder, come what may, and yet also to retain the love and respect of his people and his queen, or like Coriolanus, whose sense of his own integrity requires that he destroy Rome and his family in it so that he can, in the process, win even further approval from his mother, who will be one of the victims. Akhilleus, like these other heroes, does not see the contradiction, because he admits no limit to his passionate demands upon life. That capacity to dare to want everything, accepting fully and freely the challenge to realize all the contradictory imaginative possibilities of human experience, is the quality that sets Akhilleus apart from all the others and makes his inevitably self-destructive stance before the fatal ambiguities of experience in part a joyful affirmation of the highest ambitions of the human spirit.

IV

If the relationship with Patroklos reveals Akhilleus' most basic contact with his common humanity, then Akhilleus' extraordinary reaction to his friend's death, incomprehensible even to his peers, acquires a special importance for the reader. The death of Patroklos forces Akhilleus to realize clearly the destructive consequences of his tragic stance; the event brings on, to use Aristotle's famous term, the recognition of the fatal ironies of his heroic quest. The loss of his dearest friend opens Akhilleus' eyes fully to the consequences of his passionately individualistic striving, and for the first time he sees the inescapable and complex ambiguity of fate. The first experience of this insight overpowers Akhilleus, as it does so many tragic heroes. He hurls himself into the dust and utters a dreadful lament which echoes throughout the world (18.22). And when he rises again, he carries with him the terrible knowledge of the logic of his destiny ("I must reject this life, my heart tells me, reject the world of men" 18.90). Unlike the comic hero, who can bounce back from a fall and quickly adapt himself to a temporary setback by whatever practical means are available, Akhilleus can get up and move again only by accepting the necessary consequences of the tragic ironies of his life, only, that is, by moving a step closer to the self-destructive conclusion of his spiritual journey. When Akhilleus rises from the dust, he demonstrates that a transformation has taken place. Now he is no longer the dislocated man living totally in the sense of his apparently limitless freedom but ignorant of the truth of his condition; he gets up with the knowledge of what he must do: accept his heroic fate freely, win revenge for Patroklos, and go to his own death.

In recognizing this fact, Akhilleus, unlike anyone else in the poem, gradually comes to a mature understanding of the divinely ordained tragic suffering at the core of all human life. He sees his own conduct and the entire structure of human society from a new perspective. This vision finally has no room for the concerns of status and private anger. Akhilleus' suffering over Patroklos shows him how irrelevant those factors are to the individual who dares to stand up against fate on his own.

> *"Here I sat,*
> *my weight a useless burden to the earth,*
> *and I am one who has no peer in war*
> *among Akhaian captains--*
>
> > though in council
>
> *there are wiser. Ai! let strife and rancor*
> *perish from the lives of gods and men,*
> *with anger that envenoms even the wise*
> *and is far sweeter than slow-dripping honey,*
> *clouding the hearts of men like smoke: just so*
> *the marshal of the army, Agamémnon,*
> *moved me to anger. But we'll let that go,*
> *though I'm still sore at heart; it is all past,*
> *and I have quelled my passion as I must."* (18.104)

This wonderful speech introduces into Akhilleus' awareness a wholly new tone--one that will gradually dominate his utterances until the end of the poem--a terrible, calm resolution to carry out what he knows he must in order to be true to himself. He bids farewell to the passions that have driven him to this point, although they do not disappear yet, even if he wishes them to, acknowledges in a way we have not yet witnessed a transcendent detachment from normal human concerns, an outlook that enables him to recognize his own very human responsibility in the quarrel with Agamemnon, and accepts with an awe-inspiring finality his own imminent death. Akhilleus' tragedy has moved him into a realm beyond normal humanity, beyond even his concern for Patroklos. For in the final stages of his story, Akhilleus is not merely seeking revenge for Patroklos; if what were all, then his actions would become an absurd response to something that happens all the time in this war, as Odysseus points out in his questioning of Akhilleus' denial of the need for food before battle.

> *"So many die, so often, every day,*
> *when would soldiers come to an end of fasting?*
> *No, we must dispose of him who dies*
> *and keep hard hearts, and weep that day alone."* (19.226)

What Odysseus and the others cannot understand, however, is that Akhilleus' response to the death of Patroklos expresses much more than just his grief at the loss of a dear friend; for Akhilleus' reaction stems from his radical insight into the nature of life itself. In wanting both the common humanity symbolised in his love for Patroklos and the ultimate greatness of the passionate individual who demands his own personal accounting from fate, Akhilleus has sought the impossible. He has exposed the deepest workings of human fate. This he now recognizes. His ac-

116

tions in response to the death of Patroklos arise, therefore, out of Akhilleus' sense of the injustice of human life, which will not grant any man, no matter how intense his passions, all his deepest desires. Having unwittingly sacrificed his common humanity, Akhilleus will continue, as he must, in the lonely splendour of the man who will now pursue the mystery of fate to its centre and who, in complete freedom, accepts total responsibility for his personal confrontation with it.

The full recognition of what life means gives Akhilleus during his *aristeia* a paradoxical quality: on the one hand, he becomes extraordinarily brutal, an invincible and immoveable killing machine, free from any conventional social or emotional restraint, a man who will fight against anything that stands in his way, even the gods themselves; on the other hand, he acquires an unearthly glory, a transcendent calm, a fully mature acceptance of the mysteries of experience, unaided by the normal social rituals which shield men from a complete knowledge of their condition. The first characteristic turns Akhilleus into a human fire, inexorably destroying everything in its path; the second gives him the prophetic powers appropriate to a man who has seen deep into the heart of darkness and has returned to the world of human endeavour. Akhilleus' actions against the Trojans in battle and in the bloody sacrifice of animals and men over Patroklos' funeral pyre do not stem solely from his desire for revenge against Hektor; his wrath here he directs against the world itself, which in the absence of human love has become meaningless. Without Patroklos and what he represents, Akhilleus has no reason to live, and his remaining human passions express themselves in a cruel slaughter against everything that has disappointed his greatest hopes, including his attack on the Skamander River, against both nature and the god. If his will has come to nothing, then he will will nothingness by attacking the world as an uncompromising destroyer. At the same time, however, Akhilleus' great spiritual suffering is opening his eyes to a much more all-encompassing vision of what it means to exist as a human being.

Both of these qualities emerge in the extraordinary speech Akhilleus utters, characteristically now with "a voice of iron," in response to Lykaon's plea for mercy.

> *"Young fool, don't talk to me of what you'll barter.*
> *In days past, before Patróklos died*
> *I had a mind to spare the Trojans, took them*
> *alive in shoals, and shipped them out abroad.*
> *But now there's not a chance--no man that heaven*
> *puts in my hands will get away from death*
> *here before Ilion--least of all a son*
> *of Priam. Come, friend, face your death, you too.*

117

And why are you so piteous about it?
Patróklos died, and he was a finer man
by far than you. You see, don't you, how large
I am, and how well-made? My father is noble,
a goddess bore me. Yet death waits for me,
for me as well, in all the power of fate.
A morning comes or evening or high noon
when someone takes my life away in war,
a spear-cast, or an arrow from a bowstring." *(21.99)*

Akhilleus can dismiss Lykaon as a "fool" because he knows that plead-
ing for life in the face of death makes no sense, especially when death
comes in the form of an invincible warrior for whom the code has ceased
to exist in any meaningful way. In a world without love and companion-
ship, death is the only reality, and one who is afraid of the end of an absurd life is indeed a fool. But then, by the most wondrous turn, Akhilleus
can address his victim as "friend" and in a kind, almost avuncular tone
insist upon their common equality in the face of death. Killing and being
killed, Akhilleus now understands, belong to the inevitable order of the
universe, beyond all human custom, all system of value, all illusion-giving
conventions of status. Death, which makes all men equal, no man can
evade or transcend, not even the greatest of men who deliberately sets
himself apart. He and Lykaon are playing their parts as human beings
on this earth, according to the fatal conditions into which they were born.
That Akhilleus can declare his humanity openly with such eloquence,
here and elsewhere in his *aristeia*, while performing the killing that ends
human life, indicates just how far he has travelled into the fatal ironies
of the human condition. His urge to destroy everything, including later
the corpse of Hektor, brings out his radical dissatisfaction with life, but
his terrible composure suggests that the process of transformation continues. The difference between the normal warrior's passionate boasting and fierce preoccupation with his own status and Akhilleus' lonely,
detached calm, the awesome tranquillity of his solitary, irresistible,
aware ruthlessness, reveals the unique qualities of his present spiritual
limbo.

Not until after the killing of Hektor does Akhilleus succeed in completely emancipating himself from the passionately destructive demands
of his nature. The heroic calm breaks when he slays the Trojan hero and
savagely mutilates the corpse. And though he can finally fall asleep, he
gets no easy rest. We know from Akhilleus' attitude to Agamemnon
during the funeral rites that the traditional concerns of social man have
largely ceased to matter to him. He can make his peace with the commander-in-chief and even award him an unearned prize in the athletic
contests (23.890) because such normal concerns as status do not matter

to Akhilleus any more. The suffering he has undergone and the death which he knows awaits him have given Akhilleus a wholly different view of human experience, as a result of which the reasons for the original quarrel appear trivial. For the sake of his friend, he will observe the customary funeral rituals, but he is no longer driven by the intense search for his own personal glory. Even when he makes his request for his own tomb, he asks for nothing special ("No heavy labor at a heavy tomb I ask--only a fitting one" 23.245). Even the final reward of fame he now sees in a new light. Akhilleus here participates in the group rituals, but with a sense of their illusory nature. He will, for example, organize the games, but in some important way one gets the sense that he stands emotionally detached from the fierce striving for the honours of athletic excellence. Having seen so much into life and knowing that death is so close at hand, Akhilleus will respect traditional customs as a necessary tribute to his fellow human beings, without limiting his awareness of the fatal ironies beyond the social illusions. Not that he is yet entirely free from his old egocentric passions. So long as Hektor's body remains unburied in front of him, he cannot resist attacking it: for eleven nights he interrupts his sleep to drag the corpse around the tomb of Patroklos (24.14). Whatever calm he has gained is still threatened by the old rage.

The final stage of Akhilleus' story takes place in the encounter with Priam, in the meeting between the tragically isolated young destroyer and the long-suffering old king, both soon to perish and both filled with sorrow for the conditions of human existence. For the first time in the poem, two opponents face each other as men, not as warriors, and for all the bloody history of their antagonism, they deal as human beings first. They touch each other's real flesh, rather than trying to puncture each other's hearts with spears hurled through artistically decorated metal. No gesture in the poem is more moving than Priam's initial greeting.

> *Priam,*
> *the great king of Troy, passed by the others,*
> *knelt down, took in his arms Akhilleus' knees,*
> *and kissed the hands of wrath that killed his sons. (24.477)*

What knowledge prompts such an action? The two men share an awareness of the imperative claims of their common humanity--beyond status, riches, past exploits, or present enmity. Through the intense suffering each has experienced, they can unite momentarily in a single image of compassion for man's lot.

> *Then both were overborne as they remembered:*
> *the old king huddled at Akhilleus' feet*
> *wept, and wept for Hektor, killer of men,*
> *while great Akhilleus wept for his own father*

> *as for Patróklos once again; and sobbing*
> *filled the room. (24.509)*

And the two men, so different in all other respects, can demonstrate a mutual respect and tenderness in a shared sense of divinely ordained human grief.

> *"Come, then, and sit down.*
> *We'll probe our wounds no more but let them rest,*
> *though grief lies heavy on us. Tears heal nothing,*
> *drying so stiff and cold. This is the way*
> *the gods ordained the destiny of men,*
> *to bear such burdens in our lives, while they*
> *feel no affliction." (24.522)*

Now Akhilleus can at last surrender the corpse of Hektor. In so doing, he reaches the culmination of his tragic awareness, finally moving beyond all selfish passion into a state of pure acceptance, a state of being earned through the stages of suffering he has experienced. Revenge on the body of Hektor no longer matters. This condition is not a stoic resignation, nor is it achieved without effort, as the suggestion of the old anger indicates, when Akhilleus momentarily turns on Priam. But Akhilleus' final acknowledgement of Priam, like the old king's of him, creates a picture of their mutual awe at the ineffable mystery of life.

> *When thirst and appetite were turned away,*
> *Priam, the heir of Dárdanos, gazed long*
> *in wonder at Akhilleus' form and scale--*
> *so like the gods in aspect. And Akhilleus*
> *in his turn gazed in wonder upon Priam,*
> *royal in visage as in speech. Both men*
> *in contemplation found rest for their eyes. . . . (24.628)*

For the first time in the epic, men look at each other, say nothing, and find a temporary rest. There is nothing left for them to say or do.

To attempt to sum up the scene, and thus the epic, with a clear moral, a short prosaic phrase indicating the lesson we might derive from this tragedy would be quite inappropriate. For the climax of the *Iliad* offers us no formulaic moral instructions; it leaves us, as all great tragedy leaves us, with an overwhelming emotional sense beyond our powers of rational explanation. The experience of tragedy resists an easy moral summation because its unique power comes from the passionate complexity of the hero's ability to move beyond the ethical norms by which we customarily evaluate human life: "To experience a tragic work of art should change our lives. But give us a coherent world outlook it will not" (Lenson 171). And few remarks so instantly contradict our response to the conclusion of the *Iliad* as an attempt neatly to weigh the entire narrative according to some simple moral calculus.[9] For Akhilleus takes us into a world beyond such summary judgments. The knowledge he gains leads to his destruction, but his courage and integrity in the quest command our deepest imaginative assent. Similarly, the notion that by the end of the poem Akhilleus rediscovers his normality and resumes his previous life, as if nothing had happened to him except a temporarily unsettling experience, seriously misrepresents the emotional effect of the conclusions of the *Iliad*.[10] Akhilleus's calm at the end of the poem expresses not a return to his original normality but the spiritual readiness for death in a man who has lived as fully as any human being possibly can. Having experienced the mystery of fate, Akhilleus has nothing more to live for.

We can acknowledge the greatness of the human achievement that has gone past man's powers of rational understanding, and that is all we can say. The rest is silence. For the last genuine tribute to the dead hero can only be a mute wonder at the greatness of his human spirit. Akhilleus, of course, is not yet dead; in that sense his tragedy is unusual.[11] But after all he has been through, he has nothing left to experience. The last image pictures him sleeping peacefully. Death will come to him soon enough, and the war will continue, as before. His career has momentari-

9 For example, the following summary evaluation of the "moral deterioration" of Akhilleus: "The balance of right and wrong is depressed on the side of wrong when he rejects Agamemnon's bid for reconciliation. He rehabilitates himself and asserts the victory of civilization when he overcomes his own passionate impulse to abuse the body of Hector and returns it to Priam" (Hadas 16).

10 For example, Schein's observation that Akhilleus at the end of the epic "is reestablished as his distinctive self--as the hero he was . . . in the beginning" (162) strikes me as analogous to a claim that Macbeth's "To-morrow, and to-morrow, and to-morrow" speech reveals that, now his wife is dead, the king is really looking forward the prosperous future he faced at the start of the play.

11 Naturally, if we see in the death and funeral of Patroklos and, to a lesser extent, in the funeral of Hektor a prefiguring of the death and burial of Akhilleus, then in a sense the hero has died. It may be the case that Homer does not show Akhilleus' death in battle because the legend of his being mortally wounded by an arrow from Paris does not permit a suitably noble and tragic end, especially in a poem which holds archers in a certain contempt and which values, above all else, hand-to-hand combat. If the legend does not permit the story readily to establish a proper necessary connection between the death of the hero and his free choice, then we can admire Homer's skill all the more for giving us a sense of the death befitting the greatest of all warriors and yet without contradicting the traditional story of his death.

ly torn aside the illusions men devise to control the barbarity of nature, and he has taken upon himself the full consequences of that action. His tragic suffering alters nothing in his world, but it affirms everything about the greatest spirit of man, the striving to rise above the ironies not only of war, but of life itself.

> Without Achilles, men would have peace; without Achilles they would sleep on, frozen with boredom, till the planet itself grew cold. (Bespaloff 58)

The very last scenes in the poem depict the funeral rites for Hektor, with the traditional threnos, the lament over the body of the dead hero. Hektor here receives the immortality for which he and Akhilleus and all the warriors have striven throughout their lives, the public burial and the lasting memorial appropriate to a great hero. In that sense, Hektor's final rites sum up appropriately all the deaths we have witnessed. In the celebration around the corpse the hero enters the communal memories of his people, his greatness is assured, and he achieves the only triumph over death available to him. At the same time, however, the laments of the Trojan women over Hektor's bier remind us that the heroic career of Hektor and the tragic experience of Akhilleus, who is now waiting to die and to receive his memorial, and the deaths of all the other heroes have effected no significant changes. The war will go on; Troy will fall; the warriors will continue to fight elsewhere. That is the fate of human life, the glory and the terror, the triumph and the destruction, the paradoxical, ironic mystery from which there is no escape.[12]

---

12 To see in the funeral of Hektor a movement beyond tragedy, a final optimistic contradiction of everything we have witnessed so far, something in which "love and solidarity seem somehow more powerful than death and destruction" and which points "beyond conventional heroic values toward an ethic of humaneness and compassion" (Schein 187) is surely to sugar coat the tragic conclusion to the epic with sentimental progressivism. And given the intensity of Akhilleus' and Hektor's experiences and the ironic complexity of Homer's vision of warfare, Silk's summary judgment is, even with his later qualifications about Akhilleus, rather odd: "The Iliad is primarily celebratory, not exploratory. It presents the unchanging surface of experience, rather than the depths where nothing is constant" (102).

CHAPTER 7

Homer and the Modern Imagination

> She looked over his shoulder
>> For vines and olive trees,
> Marble well-governed cities
>> And ships upon untamed seas,
> But there on the shining metal
>> His hands had put instead
> An artificial wilderness
>> And a sky like lead.
>
> A plain without a feature, bare and brown,
>> No blade of grass, no sign of neighbourhood,
> Nothing to eat and nowhere to sit down,
>> Yet, congregated on its blankness, stood
>> An unintelligible multitude,
> A million eyes, a million boots in line,
> Without expression, waiting for a sign.
>
> Out of the air a voice without a face
>> Proved by statistics that some cause was just
> In tones as dry and level as the place:
>> No one was cheered and nothing was discussed;
>> Column by column in a cloud of dust
> They marched away enduring a belief
> Whose logic brought them, somewhere else, to grief.
>
> (W. H. Auden, "The Shield of Achilles")

I

This essay began by suggesting in Chapter 1 that a useful procedure for interpreting the English text of Homer's *Iliad* might be the notion of an unmediated conversation between the present and the past, that is, between the sensibilities of the modern reader and the apparently alien vision in Homer's text, without a preliminary excursion into the history of Ancient Greece or a study of Homer's original language or of the conventions of oral epic. The reader who has followed the essay up to this point must judge for himself if the interpretative arguments presented justify that initial assertion or not. Before concluding a discussion of the *Iliad*, however, it is appropriate in this final chapter to turn away from a close look at the text and to reflect for a few moments upon some of the reasons why this ancient poem, for all the differences between its vision of reality and ours, remains a vital part of our culture and, beyond that, can provide important imaginative assistance to us.

The enduring popularity of Homer's *Iliad* offers the most persuasive testimony of all that the vision of life celebrated in the epic still reaches deeply into the human imagination, spanning more than two thousand five hundred years, as only the greatest art can. Cultures since Homer's time, and ours is no exception, have constructed social and personal lives on systems of meaning very different from the irrational, tragic stance of the Iliadic warriors, but the continuing power of the epic reveals just how strongly the significance of that ancient way still speaks to the imaginations of men. For, to stress the main assumption on which the interpretative method in this essay rests, the *Iliad* endures, not because it qualifies as an important historical document picturing for us a civilization of human beings quite unlike modern man, but rather because it makes direct contact with the modern imagination, enabling the reader to discover, or to rediscover, those parts of his identity which contemporary visions of human nature often inadequately express or ignore altogether. To accept this interpretative assumption (not just about Homer, of course, but about all great literature from the past) is to endorse the image of each man as a microcosm of the history of human sensibility.

> When the cultural development ... of my historical moment, opens up to me the problem of Greek civilization, Platonic philosophy, or some particular phase of Attic behaviour, then that problem is as closely bound up in my being as the history of some business deal upon which I am engaged, or of some love-affair of mine, or peril overhanging me. I investigate it with the same anxiety and suffer the same sense of disgust until I manage to solve it. The life of Hellas is ... present in myself. (Croce 498)

The dialogue, then, between the past and the present, that conversation which takes place during a reading of the epic, becomes a potentially rich tension between different parts of the reader's own imagination, and the value and emotional appeal of the *Iliad* stem in very large measure from the challenge it presents to certain limits imposed by modern conventions of thought.

For today almost all readers of Homer, it goes without saying, live in a culture very different from that of Akhilleus. For one thing, we organize our personal, social, and political lives around a vision antithetical to traditional fatalism. Both capitalist and socialist democracies, as energetic offspring of the optimistic, rational, and progressive theories of the eighteenth century, accept as the major challenge to life the possibilities of changing the world continuously for the better, so that human beings can liberate themselves as quickly as possible from cosmic fate and malignant chance. And we have developed extraordinarily powerful rational metaphors which enable us to comprehend nature and the mind in such a way as to foster the central imperative of our culture. This optimistic doctrine, which one might call liberalism, informs virtually all contemporary political and personal beliefs in the West (excluding, of course, those traditional religious faiths from before the age of progress) and, with some reservations for the ambiguous component of historical determinism, Marxist ideology as well. Underlying our apparently rich array of political choices, there is a massive consensus about the appropriate relationship between man, nature, and the gods.[1]

Clearly, this liberalism encourages a faith incompatible with tragic fatalism and the conservative ethic of a static peer group. What sane modern man sets out to direct his energies in a vain fight with Zeus when all the important battles, in which victory is attainable, require him to combat the corrigible faults in his social organization or his personal life? When we substitute rational sociology or psychology for irrational fatalism, we erect a substantial imaginative barrier between ourselves and Homer. Moreover, in applying our modern scientific and mechanical models to the interpretation of human character, we have become extraordinary self-conscious. We can no longer accept actions, especially unusual departures from the norm, as simple, spontaneous expressions of character for which the agent bears no moral responsibility; instead we measure them with a formidable analytical construct which enables us to explain them away as products of this or that inner process: behind every unusual action lies an unusual molecule or a strange family life. Obviously this affects our ability to appreciate the behaviour of the Iliadic warriors; for by modern standards we too easily can see their apparently strange conduct as the action of deviants, case studies in abnormality, something to be dismissed or controlled. And the tragic hero, the man who launches himself on an ironically self-destructive quest for ultimate meaning, becomes an odd-ball. The ancient symbol of the highest possibilities for man degenerates into a clinical specimen, and tragedy vanishes from our cultural consciousness. In its place we celebrate tragicomic figures, men who cope with an emotionally absurd world by play-

---

1 My remarks on modern culture in this chapter owe a great deal to the writings of Michael Howard and George Grant.

ing absurd games, trying to fill in time until something happens, or else we laugh at or with the comic figures who retreat with style from the chaos, preoccupying themselves with contemporary fashions. The instinctual certainties of ancient tragedy have become neurotic or farcical.

Moreover, those forms of modern orthodoxy which celebrate individualism have little room for the conventions of status and public opinion as worthy guides of conduct. Inheritors of the Romantic movement, we adhere strongly to the official notion, especially in our private lives, that the individual has an obligation to create his own future and is the sole reliable evaluator of his success. The faith demands that one separate oneself from the past; the conduct of one's ancestors, if it counts at all, exists only for the individual to move beyond. Particularly in North America, where the cult of self-reliance has taken such deep root, the conservative family and peer group standards in the *Iliad* run counter to the national mythology. What cowboy hero, the ultimate self-made man, ever had parents, a home town, or a peer group to control his actions? His sense of value comes from his self-generated code of conduct, often in defiance of any group; always in motion and always alone, he defines himself, in large part, by the absence of any traditional associations. And anyway, in the large, anonymous, multi-cultural, pluralistic cities where most of the hero worshippers live, where do we find the truly significant (rather than just another stylish) peer group we need to answer to?

> Each tragic hero, in his defeat, beats on the boundaries of existence and makes them less limiting. The limits had to come from the idea of a community, where every individual had a name and a local function. This sort of community, with a system of individual craftsmanship interlocking for the common good, this pure division of labor, is a far cry from revolutionary ideas of communality or communism. These larger economies are geared to units of such massive size that every individual must be expendable. Tragedy is a remnant of the time when no one was. The older idea of community is an organic one, and the malfunction of one member of that community analogous to the failure of an organ of the body. That "body politic" has now become the "system." (Lenson 160)

To such a culture what can Homer's *Iliad* possibly say? The continuing vitality of the poem indicates that it obviously provides something significant to us, but given the radical difference between our culture's vision of life and Homer's, what could that be? In searching for an answer to this question, we discover why reading the *Iliad* matters, why the poem, for all its strangeness, generates an imaginative excitement often missing from contemporary fiction. For the *Iliad* acquaints us with potentialities of the human spirit with which we may have lost contact in daily lives shaped by a different and, in some ways, more limiting vision of reality. In doing this, the poem obviously challenges our sensibilities and forces us to explore from a fresh perspective many of those unexamined assumptions which we accept for the truth because we have never known or imagined any alternatives. If that takes place, then the epic is educating our imaginations in the fullest sense, putting us in vital contact with those parts of our human nature which our modern faith cannot entirely satisfy.

II

To accept the challenge of the Iliadic vision of human life is not always easy, for the picture Homer gives us may radically contradict our cherished faith in a very different system of order. It is not surprising, then, that the history of Homeric criticism reveals a number of different ways in which interpreters of the *Iliad* have traditionally sought to evade the challenge, that is, to transform the epic into something more readily compatible with a different vision of human existence. In such cases, the dialectical tension at the heart of the interpretative conversation becomes weighted in favour of the prejudgments and the cultural biases of the reader, and the potentially fruitful interaction between the past and the present transforms itself into a defense of the closed system of belief which the interpreter brings to bear upon Homer's text. Inevitably, such a result prevents the poem from speaking to the reader as clearly, eloquently, and usefully as it otherwise might.[2]

Some of the very earliest criticism we have of Homer, for example, finds his vision unacceptable because the religious system in the *Iliad* is incompatible with belief in a divine moral purpose or in divinities who conduct themselves in a more decorous manner than Homer depicts. The epic, in other words, for some critics presents an immoral view of existence.[3] Plato's treatment of poets, and especially of Homer, in *The Republic* is well known: they must leave the ideal state, with due honours, if their concerns are not commensurate with the rational system of belief upon which everything in the state is organized. Nowadays, the great authority of Homer as an enduring classic, the fame of his poems, means that serious critics, lacking Plato's revolutionary intentions, find it impossible firmly to dismiss the *Iliad* in this fashion, but anyone who teaches the epic to general readers will recognize a common initial response to

---

2 In this connection, it is significant that modern Homeric interpretation begins during the Enlightenment, at a time when our culture was giving birth to the progressive and rational assumptions about the nature of reality which have determined how we think about literature, the past, and human nature. Our traditions of interpretation, of Homer and others, have obviously been decisively shaped by this central cultural development.

3 "It was the things that Homer let the Gods do, not his system of theology, which roused the wrath of the educational reformers." (Myres 20)

the epic in the rejection of the poem on the ground that, by modern standards of morality, much of what it contains is abhorrent. Significantly, such a response to Homer does not always indicate, as we might too readily assume, an insensitivity to his poetry. On the contrary, the moral disapproval which the epic sometimes evokes can demonstrate that the critics are seeing and reacting to the emotional implications of Homer's vision; they are looking directly at the text of the poem. The energetic dismissal of the vision can express the urgency with which they feel the need to respond decisively to a serious threat to a different faith. Plato, in particular, strikes the reader as a critic with an extraordinary sensitivity to poetry. He treats it as he does, not because he is a totally analytical moralist, immune to Homer's beauty, but because he finds himself all too eloquently moved by the power in the verse. It is necessary to insist upon this point, because such critics often display a more honest appreciation for Homer than those who, while honoring the quality of the *Iliad*, endeavour to neutralize the challenge to a later orthodoxy.

A second strategy for dealing with the *Iliad* in such a way as to make the epic more comfortable to a different age seeks to allegorize the poem, that is, to fit the vision into a more acceptable moral scheme than Homer offers. The history of Homeric studies reveals a long tradition of such interpretation.[4] This method defends the poem against the criticisms of those who would dismiss it on moral grounds, but at the expense of forcing onto Homer's vision of experience a simpler moral paradigm which can tend to enervate the epic's most paradoxically vital centre. If the critic can draw an easy moral from the epic, subordinating its radical and discomforting ironies to an acceptably modern view, then the poem becomes an endorsement of contemporary thinking rather than a challenge to it.[5] Those interpreters who, like Don Juan's mother, earnestly wish to pass on classical learning to the young as easily and inoffensively as possible often find this method of dealing with Homer very persuasive.

> *His classic studies made a little puzzle,*
> *Because of filthy loves of gods and goddesses,*

---

4 For a very interesting study of this and related matters, see Howard Clarke. The Christian precedents for such a treatment of pagan literature are very old and authoritative, stemming, in part, from Deuteronomy 21:10, which advises the God-fearing man who wishes to domesticate a beautiful and desirable infidel enemy to "bring her home to thine house; and she shall shave her head, and pare her nails," in other words, immediately surrender all her wild, dangerous, and alluring strangeness. If she behaves herself for a while, she may stay, and an appropriately safe union may be consummated.

5 So, for example, Dryden's summary judgement in "Preface to Troilus and Cressida" that Homer's moral is "union preserves a commonwealth and discord destroys it" (1:213), or Hadas' view, quoted earlier (page 123 above), that the story of Akhilleus is a victory for civilization.

> *Who in the earlier ages raised a bustle,*
> *But never put on pantaloons or bodices;*
> *His reverend tutors had at times a tussle*
> *And for their Aeneids, Iliads, and Odysseys,*
> *Were forced to make an odd sort of apology,*
> *For Donna Inez dreaded the mythology.*

> *(Lord Byron, "Don Juan")*

An approach to the *Iliad* which seeks to transform the Trojan war into a moral encounter between the forces of civilized good and barbarian evil, for example, and which, therefore, ignores the overwhelming similarities between the opponents and the eternal, fated characteristics of the war, makes the harshness of the *Iliad* much more reassuring. We may hate the destructiveness of mortal combat as much as the ancient warriors, but the notion of a just war plays an important part in our imaginative traditions and is, indeed, one of the commonest arguments we have used for many centuries to reconcile ourselves to war's brutality. That such an interpretation of the war in the *Iliad* violates Homer's vision will be apparent to anyone who has found the arguments of this essay at all persuasive.

In a recent study of the *Iliad*, for example, Seth L. Schein presents the following view of the battle in Book Four:

> But this opening contrast between the armies begins a consistent pattern in which Homer makes the Trojans initiators not only of the battle but of the war, not merely aggressors but transgressors, who are morally responsible for their own ruin.... This symbolic reenactment of the original Trojan guilt, like their description as aggressors, effectively calls to mind the beginning of the war. (20)

This comment is surely unacceptably strained. Given the fact that the Akhaians have travelled a long way from home to raze Troy, destroy its male citizens, including the children, and to enslave the women, Schein's desire to place the war in an orthodox framework of modern belief, making it a punishment for sin, has led him to bend the notion of aggressor beyond a reasonable limit. And the description he refers to, as I have argued in Chapter 2, evokes much more strongly than any sense of moral difference the common identity and fate of the opponents, a sense consistent with the lack of a rational moral understanding in the rest of the poem. The assessment, moreover, violates the commonly expressed sympathy many readers have for the Trojans. G. S. Kirk, too, like C. M. Bowra (23), shares the view that the *Iliad* demonstrates a simple moral axiom "that all this has been made inevitable by Paris' offense against hospitality" (*Commentary* 333). Thus, the imaginative terror of Homer's gods becomes easily translated into something much more comfortable: although they are "not always Sunday-school characters in Homer, they are nevertheless determined guardians of the basic rules of order and respect" ("Homer" 73), a comment which transforms Homer's anarchic divine family into a group of those genially and mildly sadistic but, on the whole, pedagogically effective junior housemasters and housemistresses who maintain decorum in the traditional private school.

The application of a simple moralistic formula to Homer's narrative has the unfortunate effects, first, of denying that quality for which Homer has always been highly acclaimed, namely, his impersonality, the moral objectivity with which he impartially records the most passionate efforts of great men and, second, of suggesting that, far from challenging our imaginations with a sense of life's mystery, Homer has already done all the significant thinking we need to bring to the poem. Moreover, reduction of the *Iliad* to a simple morality piece does raise at least one interpretative problem which those who proffer such a reassuring hypothesis characteristically avoid. Quite apart from the persuasive evidence in the text that Zeus and his cosmic family are not driven by such a simple code, this common interpretation inevitably poses the question, familiar to readers of *Paradise Lost*: How does one reconcile such a neat moral scheme with the disproportionately harsh punishment, the destruction of an ancient city and its inhabitants, in response to the sin of romantic adultery and theft? A reasonable consideration of this issue prompted Herodotus to observe that the Greeks "were seriously to blame; for it was the Greeks who were, in a military sense, the aggressors. Abducting young women, in their opinion, is not, indeed, a lawful act; but it is stupid after the event to make a fuss about it" (42). If we are prepared to entertain the notion that the *Iliad* is principally a tale with a straightforward moral, and as critics we should be able to examine any reasonable hypothesis, then we should also be prepared to explore the interpretative implications of that hypothesis to the full and not simply use it to close off further consideration of the poem's complexities. One desiderates such a thorough critical evaluation in those who want quickly, simply, and firmly to sum up the moral framework of the *Iliad*.

One can make similar objections to other attempts to derive from the epic a picture of war more amenable to our conventional imagination; for example, Atchity's sense of the "didactic distinction" in the moralized lesson depicted on the shield of Akhilleus or Redfield's assertion that "There is not much nobility in act of war, which is in itself a negation of human things, barbaric and impure" (101). Such attempts would obviously include the strategy of distancing the reader from the heroic warriors by the use of a style rich in clinical terms, a language which establishes their extreme psychological abnormality. When, for example, critics write of the Iliadic warriors as schizophrenic and constantly subject to hallucinations (Jaynes 93) or describe Akhilleus' behaviour as "pathological barbarism" (Kirk, "Homer" 73) or "the throes of an acute neurosis" (Michelopoulos 95), the critical vocabulary may encourage readers to place the Homeric characters in that special closet we reserve for those sick people whose behaviour we find unacceptable, the hidden medical facility into which we need never glimpse. Such an interpretative language obviously inhibits the reader from exploring imaginatively the connections between his own behaviour and the often brutal irrationality of Homer's warriors. For if Homer's characters are clinically ill or psychologically abnormal, then why should we attend to them as significant human beings recognizably like ourselves?

> Our response to the Iliad can be explained as a recollection of the infantile struggle to define the self in terms of the mother's image, projected to the child, of himself, a struggle that is erotic in Freudian terms and a response to sense impression in Hegelian terms. We find in the Iliad a concentration on this narcissistic struggle and seek thereby to explain the paradox that in a poem about a war fought for a woman the focus of attention is on the relationship between the hero and his dear male companion. (MacCary xi)

The modern approach defined in the above quote inevitably leads, as one has come to expect, to the positing of an "Achilles complex" which "with its speculation of the self, if uncorrected by oedipal displacement onto others of all our ontic energy, is a vector reversing to recover that void: the death drive" (250). And so the imaginatively rich tragic suffering of Akhilleus becomes the study of yet another modern maladjusted heel.

One of the most curious and yet popular methods for neutralizing the potentially disturbing qualities of the *Iliad* leads critics to dismiss the significance of the gods on the assumption that they are merely literary devices, with no meaningful link to human reality. This tradition goes back many, many years and remains, even in this century, in spite of our vastly increased understanding of and scholarly historical interest in the vital cultural importance of "primitive" irrational religious belief, a common way of approaching a particularly difficult aspect of the epic. C. M. Bowra's well known comment defines the attitude clearly.

> This complete anthropomorphic system has of course no relation to real religion or morality. These gods are a delightful gay invention of poets who were prepared to use their material freely in an age which enjoyed its gods. (222)

This view of Homer's gods is particularly common in modern criticism of the *Iliad*: for example, John A. Scott, "The gods whom Homer pictures are not the gods she worshipped; they are poetic creations whom Homer adapted to his own needs without fear and evidently without reverence" (174); Redfield, "the gods of the *Iliad* belong to the conventional world of epic and were understood as such by the audience. Just as the epic tells not of men, but of heroes, so also it tells stories, not of gods conceived as actual, but of literary gods" (76); and West, "The gods are in general not an expression of the poet's religious beliefs but part of his mechanism for preparing future events" (17).

Clearly, this interpretative argument has a certain immediate and obvious truth: Homer's gods are literary creations in the sense that they exist in a work of literature. Unfortunately the insistence upon this point inevitably can often, implicitly or explicitly, suggest that the gods therefore have no significant relationship to serious worship and need not be taken as relevant to any meaningful understanding of human nature. Such an assumption clearly has enormously important consequences for an appreciation of the poem.

About this frequently expressed view of Homer's gods one can make a number of objections. The historical evidence sometimes adduced in support of it is necessarily very speculative, since we have no means of ascertaining reliably the relationship between Homer, his poem, and the religious beliefs or the poetical conventions of his age. And a study of Greek religion can encourage us to take the Iliadic gods as considerably more than delightful literary inventions.

> The Homeric image of divinity is an image of marvellous and compelling adequacy; it underwrites and explains the human sense of contradiction and conflict in experience, and yet contains contradiction within a more fundamental order. It enables divinity to be understood as the source of disorder in the world, and, in the extreme case, mirrored in the myth of war between the gods and giants, as the ultimate defence of order against brute chaos, as well as being the unconquerable barrier to human excess and the potentially destructive violence of human self-assertion. We would be quite wrong, I suggest, to set aside the model of divinity that we find in the Homeric poems and imagine it as a purely literary fiction and no part of the "sense" of Greek religion. (Gould 25)

Moreover, even if the historical record clearly demonstrated a significant difference between Homer's religious vision and the views of his contemporaries or established the existence of a conventional literary Olympian family, that evidence would still not necessarily mean that the Iliadic gods possessed no religious significance beyond their presence in a work of literature. For Homer, as a great artist, like Blake or Milton, is perfectly capable of creating an enduring vision at odds with contemporary orthodoxy. Our response to these deities must take its cue, surely, from the attitude developed within the poem. For example, the important difference between our assessment of, say, Milton's god in *Paradise Lost* and Pope's celestial machinery in *The Rape of the Lock* emerges not from any connection or lack of connection we may perceive between these religious visions and the historical reality of the fiction or the biographies of the authors but from the very different attitudes toward the divinities which the narrators of the poems and the characters in them express.

And whatever we may, from our contemporary perspective, think of the gods in the *Iliad*, there is no doubt that the poem takes them, even when they behave comically, very seriously indeed.

The most firmly entrenched method for separating the reader's modern sensibility from what Homer's text has to reveal of our human nature, however, is the approach which insists that we can only properly appreciate the poem if we deal with it as an ancient historical object, firmly rooted in a particular time and place, and inaccessible except to those who are willing to transport themselves back into former times, leaving behind their contemporary sensibilities. As I announced at the outset of this essay, I have no wish to weigh the conflicting theoretical demands of the past and the present, to attempt to forge a delicate path between those historical scholars, led by the ghost of Richard Bentley, for whom all talk of modern meaning smacks of rank amateurism and those interpreters, led by the ghosts of Ezra Pound and Edmund Wilson, for whom any scholarly objection to interpretive license is an unwarranted pedantic cavil. These rival camps have long been conducting an apparently interminable Trojan War of their own, and braver and more elegant spirits than I, including even Matthew Arnold, have been severely mauled in their endeavors to chart the territory appropriate to each. But any brief survey of modern treatments of the *Iliad* must take into account the ways in which the historical approach to an ancient text can, in many cases, encourage an emphasis which lessens the immediate imaginative impact of the work for the non-specialist. It may well be true, as one anonymous academic reader of this essay has objected, that "the best critics of Homer have always been historical critics, and it is quixotic to think otherwise," but it is equally true that specialized historical enquiry, for all its obvious achievements, can often tend to remove the *Iliad* from the realm of public discourse, that is, from the world of the general reader. There is no necessary reason why this reduction must happen in the study of history and literature; that it often does happen is attested to by many melancholy observations of scholars and by the curious discrepancy between the general popularity of history and Classical literature and the relatively small numbers of students who wish to pursue academic study of these fields.

> Modern studies of classical antiquity tend to stress anything and everything rather than the moral-political nexus. The present trends in classical scholarship cannot be taken as a reliable guide to either the past or the present value of the classical humanities for us.... To put it in a relatively polite and objective way, most scholarship in the humanities is not very humanistic, if measured by the value-oriented old humanities" (Else 807).

> The problem lies not in historians' methods but in their ambitions. Professionalization and specialization have reshaped history, like all academic disciplines. Historians--partly from the stark necessities of making a career, partly from a natural inclination to direct their work to those best fitted to judge--

write almost entirely for other historians (or for the students in courses taught by other historians, which in practice usually amounts to the same thing). The proliferation of more or less esoteric methodologies in the past ten or fifteen years has accelerated this tendency considerably. Countervailing pressures to speak to a wider audience of educated men and women are fitful and feeble. In this, history closely resembles other disciplines." (Turner 223-4)

The point I wish to stress here is that we must be careful not to shield ourselves from Homer with an undue emphasis upon the historical identity of the work. Of course, the *Iliad* is an immensely important historical artifact, but we must remember, too, that "As poetry [the Homeric epics] are independent of place and date, for their appeal is to human nature" (Myres 3). Thus, for example, when Whitman tells us that it is "impossible to approach the Homeric poems as one would approach the written text of any other author" (8), we need to take this advice with some care. If Whitman simply wants to call attention to Homer's unusual style, in Greek or English, then the remark states only what we might point to in any great masterpiece--its uniquely challenging poetic language. In that sense it is "impossible" to approach any masterpiece "as one would approach the written text of any other author." If, on the other hand, the claim is here, as it seems to be, that the oral conventions of Homer's poetry turn the epic into something inaccessible to the modern reader without a thorough grounding in the scanty records of oral poetry in Ancient Greek, then the general reader needs to ask himself whether he should not give up and turn his attention to appreciating Shakespeare until such time as someone tells him that understanding the plays is "impossible" without a thorough grasp of Elizabethan stage conventions and the history of blank verse. A better practice, it seems to me, is to ignore such strictures and to direct one's attention onto Homer's text in the manner I have been suggesting throughout this essay. Whitman's book, interestingly enough, refutes his own claim, for, in addition to its remarkably interesting scholarship, *Homer and the Heroic Tradition* stands out as one of the most useful and inspiring critical interpretations of the *Iliad*, very largely on the strength of the central chapters, in which Whitman quite sets aside historical concerns and approaches the text of the poem directly, in accordance with ahistorical principles of modern interpretations of English poetry, a methodology for which he offers a persuasive defense (102 ff.).[6]

6 The reference to Whitman's book prompts me to observe that, if indeed the best Homeric criticism has been carried out by historical scholars, much of the very best work comes when the scholar sets history to one side and allows his modern sensibility to interact directly with Homer's text. Nietzsche comes to mind as the most famous example of this point.

III

Given the often harsh irrationality of Homer's vision of life in the *Iliad*, we should not be surprised to see that many critics prefer to avoid facing squarely up to it. But the consequence of such a refusal to confront the discomforting strangeness of the poem is that the interpreter is denying himself the opportunity for discovering a part of his own nature, a potential insight into a fuller sense of his own humanity, and therefore a means of coming to a more mature understanding of what perplexes and frustrates him. To appreciate this point, we can examine briefly some of the ways in which the *Iliad* may throw light upon our difficulties in thinking about war. Obviously, we have a different vision of that common human activity than does the Iliadic leader. Both modern man and ancient warrior see war as an unwelcome evil, a brutal and destructive enterprise which threatens much that men strive for. In recognizing this fact, the liberal approaches war as he would any other evil, as a human problem, with particular human causes (psychological, social, political, economic, and so on) and therefore as something corrigible. He works hard to eliminate any trace of the old views that warfare is a given fact of life and that we must organize it into coherent rituals in order to make it bearable; his efforts have culminated in the twentieth-century's repeated attempts to end warfare. Every large-scale engagement he undertakes is going to be the total war to end all wars, a final crusade for peace, an enterprise for which he harnesses the entire resources of his culture. The result, even a cursory knowledge of modern history inescapably informs us, has been ironic: to multiply by the millions the destructiveness of the experience we so confidently set out to control and to leave the threat and the occurrence of warfare as common as ever. In the process, even our most humanitarian intentions have become horribly transformed into routine atrocities, and, as a result of our rational plans for the improvement of our condition, the battlefield has lost its vital human significance and turned into a place of "terrible, terrible war, made so fearful because in every country practically every man lost his head, and lost his own centrality, his own manly isolation in his own integrity, which alone keeps life real" (D. H. Lawrence 216).

> *Er nennt's Vernunft und braucht's allein,*
> *Nur tierischer als jedes Tier zu sein. (Goethe, Faust I)*[7]

---

7   "[Man] calls it reason and uses it alone/To be more of an animal than any animal."

To say this is not to suggest that Homer is right and that we are wrong. Such crude evaluations are simplistic. What our modern historical experience might suggest, however, is that our vision of war and the metaphors of human nature and society from which it springs may well be flawed in some fundamental ways which, because we are so thoroughly a product of modern times, we cannot properly comprehend. In our rational optimism, we may not be able to understand the full complexity of the most ironic of human experiences, because in some manner our cultural orthodoxy limits our ability to think about the phenomenon, because, that is, if the only tool we have is a hammer, we will inevitably tend to treat everything as if it were a nail. Looking back over the past two centuries, we can easily find plenty of evidence to suggest that many of the great slogans born in the Enlightenment were excessively sanguine. And surely none of those confident pronouncements viewed in retrospect now appears more dangerously naive than liberalism's most famous dictum about war, the heading to section twenty-four in the first chapter of *On War*, Carl von Clausewitz's classic study: "War Is Merely the Continuation of Policy by Other Means" (87). The history of combat in the one hundred and fifty years since the publication of this influential work stands as a terrible denunciation of the naive rational optimism and arrogance, in short, the hubris, revealed in those words "Merely" and "Means."[8]

To point out this obvious irony of modern times is not to claim that our utopian hopes for humankind are wholly misplaced. Nor does it mean that we must set aside our efforts to contain warfare. Who cannot applaud such a worthy ambition? However, a challenge to our conventional ways of thinking about war may well help us to recognize that many of the frustrations we encounter in dealing with it may stem, not from the complications in or misuse of Clausewitz's machine, but from the rational metaphor we apply to something which properly belongs to the mysterious and irrational order of nature, which is, in the well-known words of J. S. Haldane, not only stranger than we presently imagine, but stranger than we can possibly imagine.

We may, for example, have great trouble acknowledging Athena's presence in the battle line, in recognizing, that is, how war answers to certain powerful, joyous, and creative potentialities in the human spirit. That the best men often respond to combat with enthusiasm and a vital

---

8 Significant, too, is the industrial metaphor upon which Clausewitz bases his analysis: "The conduct of war resembles the workings of an intricate machine with tremendous friction, so that the combinations which are easily planned on paper can be executed only with great effort" (17).

pride in themselves and that the working class, which was going to save society from the cruel militarists, is often particularly eager to volunteer for the next campaign can puzzle us, often into angry denials of what we do not wish to confront, in spite of the evidence all around us. Our understanding of war, in other words, may well suffer from limited and limiting notions of human nature and providence and prevent us from a more complex sense of war's mystery. This factor might well be one of the main reasons why arguments against war which rest only on our most optimistic belief in the innate goodness and perfectibility of man, as William James recognized, are rarely effective. Commenting in 1910 on man's continuing inability to abandon warfare, James observed the following:

> Turn the fear over as I will in my mind, it all seems to lead back to two unwillingnesses of the imagination, one aesthetic, and the other moral; unwillingness, first to envisage a future in which army-life, with its many elements of charm, shall be forever impossible, and in which the destinies of peoples shall nevermore be decided quickly, thrillingly, and tragically, by force, but only gradually and insipidly by "evolution"; and, secondly, unwillingness to see the supreme theatre of human strenuousness closed, and the splendid military aptitudes of men doomed to keep always in a state of latency and never show themselves in action. These insistent unwillingnesses, no less than other aesthetic and ethical insistencies, have, it seems to me, to be listened to and respected. One cannot meet them effectively by mere counter-insistency on war's expensiveness and horror. The horror makes the thrill; and when the question is of getting the extremest and supremest out of human nature, talk of expense sounds ignominious. The weakness of so much merely negative criticism is evident-- pacificism makes no converts from the military party. The military party denies neither the bestiality nor the horror, nor the expense; it only says that these things tell but half the story. It only says that war is worth them; that, taking human nature as a whole, its wars are its best protection against its weaker and more cowardly self, and that mankind cannot afford to adopt a peace-economy. (9)

For all the questions one might want to raise about James' proposed solution to the problem (substituting a war against nature for a war against men), he has at least not evaded the central ironic difficulty of warfare, the life-affirming qualities of a brutally destructive enterprise; he brings the reader, by his own very different route, up against the complexities of nature at the centre of Homer's poem. This acceptance of the given facts of the case, the fatalistic sense of the complexities of war, it seems to me, must be the initial position for our thinking about the subject, a traditional starting point which we have, in our rational confidence, too easily dismissed. Of course, it may well contradict our dearest hopes for ourselves, but, if we wish to cope with the realities of war maturely, we must surely by now be willing to recognize the dangers of those illusions which have repeatedly disappointed us and have left us incapable of dealing intelligently with our own battle experiences.

The most obvious contemporary evidence for our inability to comprehend our own wars comes from the very popular but very confused films which attempt to make sense of the conflict in Vietnam. Remarkable about that conflict is the way in which it resists the easy moral categories our modern North American culture has developed to understand its own wars. For the first step we traditionally undertake in our response to understanding the brutality of war is to identify a particular evil person or group against whom the national forces of goodness can then direct an arsenal of liberal progress to solve the problem. We need to identify someone to blame, especially someone who, in the progressive combat between good and evil, can finally be overcome. American popular artists had no trouble fitting World Wars One and Two and the Korean War into this conventional paradigm, because the nasty Germans, Japanese, and Chinese were, in the popular imagination, so obviously the sources of all the evil which warfare brings and because the forces of goodness eventually triumphed. But the war in Vietnam is not susceptible to such treatment. The Vietnamese appear so uncomfortably close to the American vision of what constitutes goodness, and, for all the later Rambo revisionism, the Vietnamese forces emerged victorious. No one could deny the atrocities of the killing zone, and no one can yet forget the scenes of American personnel desperately scrambling for the last helicopters out of Saigon. Where did all this originate? Where is the clearly identifiable culprit? So in the popular imagination the blame lay with the liars in the White House, deranged militarists, or in some sinister military-industrial conspiracy. Even those who knew better, who were aware of the hopelessly ironic experience of the war in which the country had become enmeshed, could not challenge the national mythology which it was their political duty to sustain. Asked why he had not told the American people the truth about Vietnam, President Johnson answered with typically colloquial but revealing candour: "When your mother-in-law has only one eye and that eye is in the middle of her forehead, you don't keep her in the living room." One sees what the president meant. In the Great Society Polyphemos is not a native son, or at least we do not openly admit to a relationship. The optimistic national faith in the goodness of man and the country does not wish to confront a more sinister vision of itself; it wants, by contrast, to protect itself with "the illusions of eternal strength and health, and of the essential goodness of people; illusions of a nation, the lies of generations of frontier mothers who had to croon falsely, that there were no wolves outside the cabin door" (F. S. Fitzgerald 134). In the Vietnam experience, the wolves came right into the house, and ever since, following President Johnson's advice, American popular artists have been trying to shove them into a hidden back room.

Such widely hailed films as *Apocalypse Now* (1979), *Platoon* (1987), *Full Metal Jacket* (1987), and *Good Morning, Vietnam* (1988), for example, depict graphically enough the horrors of war; in fact, the single most remarkable quality of these films is their rendition of the grinding and bloody interaction between men and matter, and the most compelling moments arise out of the powerful images of the destructive machinery of war. But to judge from these films (and others), the director lacks any significant way of making sense out of this destruction. The obsession with the material face of war often suggests that the director is hoping that a coherent human response to the experience will emerge somehow or other from a faithful rendition of the brutal surface details. The frequent and unsatisfactory use (by now a familiar convention) of the coordinating central monologue by the main character to link the scenes only reminds us how impossible it is for any American Everyman to remain true to his national faith and, at the same time, to recognize the fatal ambiguities of conduct to which the depictions of war call attention.

In other words, these films, by providing naturalistic pictures of men in battle, immediately raise certain very complex questions about the nature of warfare, but then, as if ignorant of or horrified by what is emerging, the films inevitably display no intelligent awareness of the ironies which they themselves (unintentionally or not) reveal. An obvious example occurs in *Platoon*, which rather crudely directs the viewer to accept Sergeant Elias as evil and Sergeant Barnes as good. But the film necessarily raises a question it does not dare to explore: Why, then, is the good man doing exactly the same thing as the bad man, killing the enemy and leading his men out to be killed? And why, for all his protestations to the contrary, does he appear to be so good at it and to enjoy himself so much? Quite against the director's conscious intentions, the "evil" Sergeant Elias emerges as the only character of real depth and interest in the film, because he is the only one who looks directly at the war and makes a considered decision to accept it as a condition of his life, since he cannot escape it, and to impose his will upon it, rather than constantly trying to evade it or to complain with a string of colloquial and repetitive obscenities. *Apocalypse Now* neutralizes any imaginative discomfort by presenting the central character, Willard, as abnormal right from the opening frames, a man who sleeps beside his gun and slashes his own flesh as part of his morning ablutions. The violence is shocking, but the image finally consoling: whatever happens on the strange trip up the river need not affect the viewer's sense of himself, because clearly Willard is, like Colonel Kurtz, a freak. And Willard does not have to deal with anything he might have learned from his nightmarish trip because the film leaves him stranded, miles up a foreign creek, while napalm takes care of the horror he has experienced. *Good Morning, Vietnam* brings the protagonist right up against some of the complexities of war, including the awareness of his own complicity in the violence, and then forcibly removes him from having to act on his awareness, easily and evasively resolving his problems with a silly baseball game and laying the blame for the evils of war on stupid military types. He does not have to evaluate and act upon his new knowledge because by the time he finds out what is really going on, he knows he is going home.

In adopting such evasive strategies, whatever their declared intentions about delivering the reality of the war, many modern film-makers are really trying, and to judge from the public approval for their efforts, evidently succeeding, in consoling the audience, in demonstrating with sentimental popular art that the liberal vision is still intact and that but for a few nasty militarists, mentally unbalanced citizens, and sleazy politicians, the Vietnam war would never have happened. By striving to put the war behind America, into the quickly forgotten past, the films resurrect the frontier lies and reassure their audiences that the wolves have migrated elsewhere. Responding to the optimistic imperatives of the national consciousness, the film-makers dissolve Homer's front-line sibling partnership of Athena and Ares, convert Athena into a lover of peace (or, more commonly, a hater of war), keep Ares, now the orphan result of some inexplicable and unwelcome lethal recessive mutation in the shape of a few particular human beings, and set the two deities against each other, finally awarding the palm to Athena. In the process, for all the full-screen horror these films depict, the harsh, irrational fatalism of warfare becomes changed into a reasonable, comforting, and sentimental moral allegory.

The imaginative failure of the American popular culture to comprehend its own experience of war emerges also in the great hostility which often greets attempts to explore the phenomenon in more complex ways than the films mentioned above. Cimono's film *Deer Hunter*, for example, makes an unusual and intelligent attempt to picture the connections between the experience of combat and the warrior's origins in and his return to a community governed by traditional ritual. Although in the film the connections between that community and the war are very tenuous, Cimono's treatment of the effects of war and especially his very disturbing and powerful central metaphor of Russian roulette offer no easy moral triumph for the American way; indeed, at the end of the film the communal singing of "God Bless America" reveals the thinness of the national sentiment when matched against the irrational absurdity of the experiences we have witnessed. But liberal apologists routinely castigate the film with charges of xenophobic "racism" and "political amnesia," largely because Cimono shows the Vietnamese soldiers caught up in the barbarous treatment of prisoners-of-war. And thus the potential illumination of some aspects of war's complexity gets shoved aside while opponents of this critical vision debate the historical veracity of Cimono's narrative (see, for example, "Four Shots" and Kael 512-519). Similarly, *The Warriors* (1979), not a Vietnam film but a particularly interesting exploration of urban combat, earned the wrath of Sol Yurick, the Marxist-inspired author of the book on which the film was based. He hated the film because it had taken his vision of the economic deprivation of the young New York street gangs, an attack on the social imperfections of American society--"You see, I wanted to get across the sense of what the social distribution of wealth really means" (qtd Auster and Georghkas 22)--and turned it into a challenging picture of how in the midst of an irrational, hostile, and fated labyrinth, from which there is no exit and where danger leaps out from every corner, the human spirit responds with a Homeric sense of aggressively brutal and frequently beautiful individualistic assertiveness, held together by the dynamics of status within the group. The author's liberal imagination could not accept the Greekness of the film. That was odd, of course, because he had based his story on Xenophon's *Anabasis*.

IV

To introduce into an essay on Homer's *Iliad* a discussion of modern visions of battle is a legitimate means of calling attention to a central argument of this essay, namely, that Homer's epic has much to teach us about ourselves. For a culture's vision of war, the way its people comprehend that universal experience, arises out of its deepest assumptions about man, nature, and the gods, that is, from the mythology basic to the way people think and feel. One is not surprised, therefore, to see that the difficulties popular film-makers have in exploring the Vietnam conflict are to a large extent shared by intellectuals investigating the same events. The academic literature on that war, by now very copious, demonstrates again and again the extent to which the attempts to understand what happened and why are limited by the liberal assumptions about the nature of man fundamental to our intellectual enquiries. The terrible emotional impact of a brutal war and a humiliating defeat are explained away in accounts of the events which point to the unskillful use of the machinery of war, the evil or stupidity of particular leaders, the ignorance of those who should have studied the data more thoroughly, and so on. Significantly absent is the notion that warfare is something beyond complete human control and understanding and that, therefore, the confidence with which we discuss it and try to use it as "Merely the Continuation of Policy by Other Means" or as a machine with lots of friction reveals a dangerous naivete which we would be wise to take into account. Such studies thus not only prevent us from recognizing any possible connection between the destructiveness, our inadequate metaphors, and the mysterious passions lurking in nature, but also finally reassure us: there is nothing intrinsically wrong with the metaphor or with the common man; we (or some of us) just applied it incorrectly.[9] And, after all, the Vietnamese never beat us in a pitched battle.

To those who maintain such a comforting hypothesis the example of Senator William Fulbright is particularly instructive. In his opposition to the Vietnam expedition, Senator Fulbright was fond of pointing out the parallels between American folly and Thucydides' account of the Athenian expedition to Sicily. The comparison is obviously pertinent, in the same way that a comparison with Homer's vision of the Trojan war is pertinent, for it calls attention to the ironic disparity between the fondest hopes of ambitious, naive, and overconfident human beings and the eternally mysterious reality of nature, human and non-human. One wonders, however, what might have happened in the congressional debates on Vietnam if Senator Fulbright, the most authoritative spokesman in Congress on matters of foreign policy at the time, had attended to Thucydides earlier, before he began his opposition to the war, before, that is, he personally sponsored, in August 1964, the Gulf of Tonkin resolution, which gave the American intervention whatever national legitimacy it possessed.[10]

It is clear that on the basis of those assumptions which inform how they think and feel, men determine the most important choices in their personal, social, and political lives. So long as we restrict ourselves to the conventions in which we have been educated to perceive reality, our ability fully to grasp what we are is, in some essential manner, limited, for we have no proper way of understanding, let alone dealing with, problems which arise out of the very concepts we use to interpret nature, including our own. The *Iliad* remains important and valuable to us, not because it provides us with a viable alternative system of belief, but because it puts great pressure on us to examine the adequacy of our conventional ways of thinking and feeling. That human beings can often

9 See Smith, "Vietnam Without Fear" and "Vietnam Post Mortem."
10 The resolution, it is worth remembering, passed unanimously in the House after only forty minutes of debate. In the Senate only two dissenting voices were heard: Senators Morse of Oregon and Gruening of Alaska. Senator Fulbright, who regretted his decision ever after, claimed that the President had lied to him. Both Homer and Thucydides, in their different ways, would have informed the Senator clearly enough that in matters of warfare, folly and lies in high places are not unusual. See Baritz (140-143).

respond powerfully to uncomfortable visions which challenge their favorite ideas is evident in the popularity of Homer's epic, which, in spite of the fact that many interpretations seek to blunt that challenge, remains an imaginatively rich and moving vision. This force of a different view of nature stands revealed also in the most extraordinary and eloquent legacy of the Vietnam experience: the memorial in Washington, D.C., to the Vietnam dead. For this tribute to the victims of the war, designed by Maya Lin, is anything but a conventional monument neatly deposited on an appropriate civic square, a tidy white decoration celebrating with a suitable *pro patria mori* slogan the valour and patriotism of the slain. The black Vietnam wall rises from the earth like some grimly beautiful chthonian presence announcing the secret and bloody powers of nature itself. The contrast between it and the neighboring Washington Monument and Lincoln Memorial, with which the shape of the wall deliberately links itself, could hardly be more striking. Not surprisingly, the design met fierce opposition to what conventional thinking, accustomed to very different tributes to the fallen, labelled a "black gash of shame," something "unheroic, unpatriotic, below ground, and death oriented" (Swerdlow 563). That the design could survive the selection process intact with only minor modifications is a tribute to the emotional richness of the stark image. Extraordinary, too, is the feeling the memorial creates in the visitors who approach it, a reaction quite different from the typical response to traditional cenotaphs. At the Vietnam wall, those close to it feel impelled to touch the stone or kiss it, as if they wish quite spontaneously to establish an irrational but vital contact between the earth out of which the stone has come and their own frail lives. No purely rational analysis of the Vietnam conflict even understands let alone communicates a sense of the atavistic truth which emerges from that stone and ground.

> *In spite of all our needs*
> *we do help at her labors.*
> *We deliver bodies to fertilize the body we fight over.*
> *We die to make bodies count for something,*
> *to control the places of slaughter*
> > *that the old terror we still call Mother*
> > *in the earth wind and water*
> > *intended as field of praise. (Gerald Barrax)*

There is surely no profounder public symbol of the challenge to modern Western man than the images honoring the ideals of George Washington, the founder of the nation, the eloquent and courageous striving of Abraham Lincoln, the preserver of the union, and the mysteriously beautiful and ominous powers of the earth itself, all in close proximity in the political heart of the Western enterprise. Our future will be determined more than anything else by the extent to which we can in our public and personal lives manifest and combine the paradoxical qualities of human life that those monuments, all of them, reveal and preserve, recognizing that we must retain our faith in the ideals that lift our eyes up to the sky, that we must fight to defend the best hopes for man, and, finally and most important, that in seeking life, liberty, and the pursuit of happiness for all, we put those very ideals at terrible risk whenever we neglect the ancient and powerful forces which still, whether we care to acknowledge them or not, ascend irresistibly out of the earth to impose limits upon our most cherished visions of ourselves.

To be put back into imaginative touch with the irrational centres of human life is to experience the fullest and maturest awareness of our most vital hopes. For only by testing those hopes against alternative visions can we properly understand a little better than we do the conditions common to us all.

> So long as we see our troubles exclusively from the familiar cultural, anthropocentric perspective, they can appear only as problems awaiting a technical or political solution. But what if we tried not so much to overcome our problems as to understand them and listen to what is speaking there? Nothing in today's civilization encourages so seemingly passive a stance, but if we were able sometimes to look at our situation through older eyes and with their aid relearn the power of limit (the limes or boundary line separating the human settlement from the wild, whose encroachments must always be respected), then the more equable relation between culture and nature which some are looking for might seem less unattainable. A search into our past might prove to be not a step back but a way of facing the questions that come at us from the future. (Carne-Ross 60)

One final point. In recent years, we have been witnessing in North America a cultural crisis, a loss of confidence in the Western enterprise and an increasing confusion about the value of our civilization. As our power over human and non-human nature grows exponentially, so, too, it seems, do our doubts. Many of those who have written recently about this malaise (E. D. Hirsch, Jr., Alan Bloom, Gerald Graff, and Christopher Lasch, for example) from many different intellectual perspectives echo the words in the above quote, seeing in our neglect of the past the source of our confusion and in a rediscovery of that cultural past the very best hope we have for regaining a sense of a purposeful present and future.

> Our culture's indifference to the past--which easily shades over into active hostility and rejection--furnishes the most telling proof of that culture's bankruptcy. The prevailing attitude, so cheerful and forward-looking on the surface, derives from a narcissistic impoverishment of the psyche and also from an inability to ground our needs in the experience of satisfaction and contentment.... A denial of the past, superficially progressive and optimistic, proves on closer analysis to embody the despair of a culture that cannot face the future. (Lasch 25)

I share the conviction that our best hopes for the future must emerge, not from a more energetic recommitment to further inventions, utopian revolutions, therapeutic strategies, technological innovations, or narcotic anodynes, but rather from an imaginative re-engagement with our neglected traditions. My purpose in writing this essay has been to encourage the reader to see in the *Iliad*, in its beauty, power, and terror, a uniquely rich vision of human nature which can reacquaint us with ourselves, with that joy and wonder of tragic striving in the face of destiny, a response which may still summon from us the courage to realize more fully and intelligently what we can be, in an age that often, it seems, in the effort to liberate man, has somehow sadly reduced his significance.

LIST OF WORKS CITED

This list includes only those works cited in the text and footnotes. It is not, therefore, a general introductory bibliography of works on Homer's *Iliad*. Readers seeking such a bibliography should consult the books by Mueller, Silk, or Schein listed below.

Aichinger, Peter. *The American Soldier in Fiction, 1880-1963*. Ames, Iowa: Iowa University Press, 1975.

Armstrong, Paul. "The Conflicts of Interpretations and the Limits of Pluralism." *PMLA* 98.3 (May 1983): 341-352.

Atchity, Kenneth John. *Homer's Iliad: The Shield of Memory*. Carbondale and Edwardsville: Southern Illinois University Press, 1978.

Auerbach, Erich. *Mimesis*. Translated Willard Trask. Garden City: Doubleday, 1957.

Auster, Al and Dan Georghkas. "The Warriors: An Interview with Sol Yurick." *Cinéaste* 9.3 (Spring 1979): 22-24.

Baritz, Loren. *Backfire: A History of How American Culture Led Us into Vietnam and Made Us Fight the Way We Did*. New York: William Morrow, 1985.

Bespaloff, Rachel. *On the Iliad*. Translated Mary McCarthy. Princeton: Princeton University Press, 1947. Rep. 1970.

Bowra, C. M. *Tradition and Design in the Iliad*. Oxford: Clarendon Press, 1930. Reprinted Westport: Greenwood Press, 1977.

Burnett, John. *Early Greek Philosophy*. New York: Meridian, 1957.

Carne-Ross, D. S. "The Beastly House of Atreus." *Kenyon Review* N.S. 3.2 (Spring 1981): 20-60.

Clarke, Howard. *Homer's Readers: A Historical Introduction to the Iliad and the Odyssey*. Newark: University of Delaware Press, 1981.

Clausewitz, Carl von. *On War*. Edited and Translated by Michael Howard and Peter Paret. Princeton: Princeton University Press, 1976.

Croce, Benedetto. *Philosophy Poetry History*. Translated by Cecil Sprigge. London: Oxford University Press, 1966.

Dodds, E. R. *The Greeks and the Irrational*. Berkeley: University of California Press, 1973.

Dryden, John. *The Essays of John Dryden*. Selected and edited by W. P. Ker. In 2 vols. New York: Russell & Russell, 1961.

Else, Gerald F. "The Old and the New Humanities." *Daedalus* 8.3 (Summer 1969): 803-808.

Fitzgerald, F. Scott. *Tender is the Night*. New York: Scribner's, 1933.

Fitzgerald, Robert, trans. *The Iliad*. New York: Anchor Press/Doubleday, 1975.

---. "Heroic Poems in English." *Kenyon Review* 14.4 (Autumn 1952): 698-706.

"Four Shots at *The Deer Hunter*." *Film Quarterly* 32.4 (Summer 1979): 10-22.

Ginsberg, Robert, editor. *The Critique of War*. Chicago: Henry Regenry, 1969.

Gould, John. "On making sense of Greek religion." *Greek Religion and Society*. Edited P. R. Easterling and J. V. Muir. Cambridge: Cambridge University Press, 1985. Reprinted 1986: 1-33.

Graff, Gerald. *Literature Against Itself: Literary Ideas in Modern Society*. Chicago: Chicago University Press, 1979.

Grant, George. *Technology and Empire: Perspectives on North America*. Toronto: Anansi, 1969.

Griffin, Jasper. *Homer*. New York: Hill and Wang, 1980.

Griffiths, Trevor. *Comedians*. New York: Grove Press, 1976.

Hadas, Moses. *A History of Greek Literature*. New York: Columbia University Press, 1950.

Herodotus. *The Histories*. Translated Aubrey de Sélincourt. Revised A. R. Burn. Harmondsworth: Penguin, 1972.

Herr, Michael. *Dispatches*. New York: Avon Books, 1980.

Howard, Michael. *War and the Liberal Conscience*. New Brunswick: Rutgers University Press, 1978.

Hughes, Robert. "Gold of the Nomads." *Time*. 21 April 1975: 54.

James, William. "The Moral Equivalent of War." *War and Morality*. Edited by Richard Wasserstrom. Belmont: Wadsworth, 1970: 4-14.

Jaynes, Julian. *The Origins of Consciousness in the Breakdown of the Bicameral Mind*. Boston: Houghton Mifflin, 1976.

Kael, Pauline. "The God-Bless-America Symphony." *When the Lights Go Down*. New York: Holt, Reinhart and Winston, 1980: 512-519.

Keegan, John. *The Face of Battle*. Harmondsworth: Penguin Books, 1978.

Kerr, Walter. *Tragedy and Comedy*. New York: Simon and Schuster, 1967.

Kirk, G. S. *The Songs of Homer*. Cambridge: Cambridge University Press, 1962. Rep. 1977.

---. "Homer." *The Cambridge History of Classical Literature: I: Greek Literature*. Edited by P. E. Easterling and B. M. W. Knox. Cambridge: Cambridge University Press, 1985: 42-91.

---. *The Iliad. A Commentary: Volume I: books 1-4*. Cambridge: Cambridge University Press, 1985.

Kisiel, Theodore. "The Happening of Tradition: The Hermeneutics of Gadamer and Heidegger." *Hermeneutics and Praxis*. Edited Robert Hollinger. Notre Dame, Indiana: University of Notre Dame Press, 1985: 3-31.

Knight, Douglas. *Pope and the Heroic Tradition: A Critical Study of His Iliad*. New Haven: Yale University Press, 1951.

Krieger, Murray. *The Classic Vision: The Retreat from Extremity*. Baltimore: Johns Hopkins University Press, 1973.

Lasch, Christopher. *The Culture of Narcissism*. New York: Warner Books, 1979.

Lattimore, Richard, trans. *The Iliad of Homer*. Chicago: University of Chicago Press, 1951.

Lawrence, D. H. *Kangaroo*. London: Heinemann, 1923. Rep. 1974.

Leitch, Vincent B. "The Lateral Dance: The Deconstructive Criticism of J. Hillis Miller." *Critical Inquiry* 6.4 (Summer 1980): 593-607.

Lenson, David. *Achilles' Choice: Examples of Modern Tragedy*. Princeton: Princeton University Press, 1975.

MacCary, W. Thomas. *Childlike Achilles: Ontology and Phylogeny in the Iliad*. New York: Columbia University Press, 1982.

Michalopoulos, Andre. *Homer*. New York: Twayne, 1966.

Monro, D. B. *Homeri Opera et Reliquiae*. Oxford: Clarendon Press, 1896.

Mueller, Martin. "Knowledge and Delusion in the *Iliad*." *Essays on the Iliad: Selected Modern Criticism*. Edited John Wright. Bloomington: Indiana University Press, 1978: 105-123.

---. *The Iliad*. London: George Allen & Unwin, 1984.

Myres, Sir John L. *Homer and His Critics*. Edited Dorothea Gray. London: Routledge and Kegan Paul, 1958.

Paley, F. A. *The Iliad of Homer, with English Notes*. In 2 vols. London: George Bell, 1866.

Rabkin, Norman. "Meaning and Shakespeare." *Shakespeare 1971*. Edited Clifford Leech and J. M. R. Margeson. Toronto: University of Toronto Press, 1972: 89-106.

Redfield, J. M. *Nature and Culture in the Iliad: The Tragedy of Hector*. Chicago: University of Chicago Press, 1975.

Richardson, N. J. "Early Greek views about life after death." *Greek Religion and Society*. Edited by P. E. Easterling and J. V. Muir. Cambridge: Cambridge University Press, 1985. Reprinted 1986: 50-66.

Rieu, E. V., trans. *The Iliad*. Harmondsworth: Penguin Books, 1950.

Russo, Joseph and Bennett Simon. "Homeric Psychology and Oral Epic Tradition." *Essays on the Iliad: Selected Modern Criticism*. Edited John Wright. Bloomington: Indiana University Press, 1978: 41-57.

Schein, Seth L. *The Mortal Hero: An Introduction to Homer's Iliad*. Berkeley: University of California Press, 1984.

Scott, John A. *The Unity of Homer*. New York: Biblo and Tannen, 1965.

Silk, Michael. *Homer: The Iliad*. Cambridge: Cambridge University Press, 1987.

Simon, Bennett. *Mind and Madness in Ancient Greece: The Classical Roots of Modern Psychiatry*. Ithaca: Cornell University Press, 1978.

Smith, Geoffrey S. "Vietnam Without Fear." *Queen's Quarterly* 90.4 (Winter 1983): 972-982.

---. "Vietnam Post-Mortem." *Queen's Quarterly* 94.2 (Summer 1987): 415-426.

Swerdlow, Joel L. "To Heal a Nation." *National Geographic* 167.5 (May 1985), 555-573.

Turner, James. "Recovering the Uses of History." *The Yale Review* 70.2 (Winter 1981): 221-233.

Vivante, Paolo. *The Homeric Imagination: A Study of Homer's Poetic Perception of Reality.* Bloomington: Indiana University Press, 1970.

Voltaire. *Candide.* Translated and edited by Robert M. Adams. New York: Norton, 1966.

Weil, S. *The Iliad or the Poem of Force.* Translated M. McCarthy. Pendle Hill Pamphlets, no 91. Wallingford, Pennsylvania, 1957.

West, M. L. "Homeric and Hesiodic poetry." *Ancient Greek Literature.* Ed. K. J. Dover. Toronto: Oxford University Press, 1980: 10-28.

Whitman, Cedric H. *Homer and the Homeric Tradition.* New York: Norton, 1965.

Wilkinson, Elizabeth M. and L. A. Willoughby, trans. and edd. *On the Aesthetic Education of Man: in a Series of Letters.* Oxford: Clarendon Press, 1967.

Willcock, M. M. "Some Aspects of the Gods in the *Iliad.*" *Essays on the Iliad: Selected Modern Criticism.* Edited John Wright. Bloomington: Indiana University Press, 1978: 58-69.

---. *A Companion to the Iliad.* Chicago: University of Chicago Press, 1976.

---. *A Commentary on Homer's Iliad, Books I-VI.* London: Macmillan, 1970.

Wimsatt, W. K. "Genesis: A Fallacy Revisited." *Issues in Contemporary Literary Criticism.* Edited Gregory T. Polletta. Boston: Brown and Company, 1973: 255-276.

Wright, John. *Essays on the Iliad: Selected Modern Criticism.* Bloomington: Indiana University Press, 1978.

Index

Ian C. Johnston is an instructor at Malaspina College, Nanaimo, British Columbia, where he teaches Technical Writing, English Literature and Composition, and Classical Literature in Translation.